Ha[ ]day
to th[ ]g
aunt a niece could
ask for! I love you!
Love,
Lauren

January 1, 2023

"No one in the evangelical world has done more reading, thinking, praying, and reflecting on suffering and faith than Joni Eareckson Tada. She is always 'must-reading,' but this particular book is a brilliant addition to her body of work. Music sends theology deep into the heart in a unique way, and Joni's meditations on these beautiful hymns will make them even more effective in your life. Highly recommended."

TIM KELLER, Pastor Emeritus, Redeemer Presbyterian Church, New York City

"Scripture tells us to be Spirit-filled, 'addressing one another in psalms and hymns and spiritual songs, singing and making melody to the Lord with your heart.' Joni is the only person I know who actually lives this out, and she does it despite suffering more than anyone else I know. God has given Joni to the church as a gift and beautiful example of sacrificial worship. I'm so grateful that she has authored this book!"

FRANCIS CHAN, Crazy Love Ministries; Pastor; author, *Crazy Love* and *Letters to the Church*

"Once again Joni has found a way to redeem her suffering and to do so in a way that inspires and encourages others. A gorgeous book with a deep message."

PHILIP YANCEY, author, *Where the Light Fell* and *What's So Amazing About Grace?*

"My friend Joni lives with pain in her body, a tune in her heart, and a song on her tongue. Her faithful ministry to us all comes through the songs she sings, the great example of what Ephesians 5:19 was meant to look like in us all. I aspire to become what I see in my sister. In her prolonged suffering, she worships her loving Father to proclaim his greatness to a watching world. Joni is a miracle, a spectacle of grace. Who better to lead us through our most precious hymns for the hardest seasons of life?"

TONY REINKE, Senior Teacher; Host, *Ask Pastor John*, Desiring God

"Joni is a pillar of hope to our generation. I'm grateful for her wisdom and for her voice that cuts through the complacency and calls us to hope. This devotional collection is one you'll reach for when you're weary."

SANDRA MCCRACKEN, singer-songwriter; hymn writer; recording artist; columnist, *Christianity Today*; author, *Send Out Your Light*

"*Songs of Suffering* is one of those rare books that isn't intended to be read; it's intended to be experienced. I sang, cried, smiled, prayed, and worshiped through every page. No matter what you're walking through, let Joni be your song leader, and your heart won't be the same."

DAVID PLATT, Pastor-Teacher, McLean Bible Church; author, *Radical: Taking Back Your Faith from the American Dream*

"Where would we be without hymns? Where would we be without songs to express our sorest griefs and deepest sorrows? I hope you'll allow Joni Eareckson Tada to introduce you to some of the best and most powerful of them all, to explain how they have been a blessing and comfort to her—and to encourage you to get to know them, to commit them to memory, and to sing them before the Lord, so they can be a blessing and comfort to you as well."

TIM CHALLIES, author, *Seasons of Sorrow*

"If you take the time to open up this book, be warned: it will grow your faith. It will help you fall in love with Christ more, as you learn to sing hymns that will sustain you and uphold you through days of misery and suffering. I was greatly encouraged by Joni's *Songs of Suffering, and you will be too.*"

DEEPAK REJU, Pastor of Biblical Counseling and Family Ministry, Capitol Hill Baptist Church, Washington, DC

"Joni's gorgeous writing, as poetic as the hymns she champions and cherishes, helped me stare into the time-honored texts, many of which I've sung all my life, and discover depths and beauties I'd not seen before. Reading this book was truly illuminating and inspiring to my heart."

FERNANDO ORTEGA, hymn writer; recording artist; worship leader

"Joni has given us a gift: to learn to sing through our sorrows and all the days of our lives. Through historical hymns and biblical reflections, we are reminded to go to our Savior, who cares for us more deeply than we could ever imagine. Join Joni and the choir of those who have gone before us to sing of the excellencies of our God. Your heart will be glad as your tongue rejoices (Ps. 16:9)."

TRILLIA NEWBELL, author, *A Great Cloud of Witnesses*; *If God Is For Us*; and *Sacred Endurance*

SONGS *of* SUFFERING

25 Hymns and Devotions for Weary Souls

Joni Eareckson Tada

Foreword by Keith and Kristyn Getty

CROSSWAY®

WHEATON, ILLINOIS

Songs of Suffering: 25 Hymns and Devotions for Weary Souls
Copyright © 2022 by Joni Eareckson Tada
Published by Crossway
          1300 Crescent Street
          Wheaton, Illinois 60187

Published in association with the literary agency of Wolgemuth & Associates, Inc.

The poem stanza cited in the foreword is from "David's Crown" by Malcolm Guite, Canterbury Press 2021, used with the author's permission.
"O Church, Arise" by Stuart Townend and Keith Getty. Copyright © 2005 Thankyou Music (PRS) (adm. worldwide at CapitolCMGPublishing.com excluding the UK & Europe which is adm. at IntegratedRights.com) All rights reserved. Used by permission.

Cover Design: Jordan Singer
Cover Photo: Tim Kellner
Photographs copyright © 2022 by Crossway

First printing 2022

Printed in China

Unless otherwise indicated, Scripture quotations are from the ESV® Bible (The Holy Bible, English Standard Version®), copyright © 2001 by Crossway, a publishing ministry of Good News Publishers. Used by permission. All rights reserved.
Scripture quotations marked NIV are taken from the Holy Bible, New International Version®, NIV®. Copyright © 1973, 1978, 1984, 2011 by Biblica, Inc.™ Used by permission of Zondervan. All rights reserved worldwide. www.zondervan.com. The "NIV" and "New International Version" are trademarks registered in the United States Patent and Trademark Office by Biblica, Inc.™
Scripture quotations marked NLT are taken from the Holy Bible, New Living Translation, copyright © 1996, 2004, 2015 by Tyndale House Foundation. Used by permission of Tyndale House Publishers, a Division of Tyndale House Ministries, Carol Stream, Illinois 60188. All rights reserved.

All emphases in Scripture quotations have been added by the author.

Trade paperback ISBN: 978-1-4335-7640-9
ePub ISBN: 978-1-4335-7643-0
PDF ISBN: 978-1-4335-7641-6
Mobipocket ISBN: 978-1-4335-7642-3

Library of Congress Cataloging-in-Publication Data

Names: Tada, Joni Eareckson, author. | Getty, Kristyn, writer of foreword.
Title: Songs of suffering : 25 hymns and devotions for weary souls / Joni Eareckson Tada ;
    foreword by Kristyn Getty.
Description: Wheaton : Crossway, 2022. | Includes bibliographical references and index.
Identifiers: LCCN 2021049795 (print) | LCCN 2021049796 (ebook) | ISBN 9781433576409 (trade paperback) | ISBN
    9781433576416 (pdf) | ISBN 9781433576423 (mobi) | ISBN 9781433576430 (epub)
Subjects: LCSH: Suffering—Religious aspects—Christianity. | Music—Religious aspects—Christianity. | Consolation.
Classification: LCC BV4909 .T26 2022 (print) | LCC BV4909 (ebook) | DDC 248.8/6—dc23/eng/20211130
LC record available at https://lccn.loc.gov/2021049795
LC ebook record available at https://lccn.loc.gov/2021049796

Crossway is a publishing ministry of Good News Publishers.

RRDS			32	31	30	29	28	27	26	25	24	23	22
14	13	12	11	10	9	8	7	6	5	4	3	2	

For Rika Theron

The night of this little dark world is already quickly passing away. The dawn of eternity will soon appear, and then the King's own voice will speak. And every "prisoner of hope"— the afflicted and the struggling ones—will stand forth—emancipated and unhurt—the brighter, the gladder, and the more beloved for all the sufferings through which they passed. And there, they will magnify God's holy name for the salvation He wrought. And as each faithful spirit goes up to its eternal rest, and his foes are at His feet for ever—this will be all his history, and all his boast—"He believed in his God."[1]

This will be all your history, Rika, and all your boast— "She believed in her God."

Your statutes have been my songs
in the house of my sojourning.
—PSALM 119:54

Contents

PART 2: SONGS OF STRENGTH

PART 3: SONGS OF HOPE

Personal Reflections from the Gettys

"Joni, will you ever walk again?" Eliza's little six-year-old eyes were earnestly fixed upon her. With her clear blue eyes sparkling back Joni replied, "Yes, I will! When I go to see Jesus in heaven, he will give me new legs, and I will walk again." We moved out into the street after that and, walking beside her wheelchair toward the parking lot, began to sing, "Soon and very soon we are going to see the King." Great hope sung along a little street in Pasadena, California.

You always sing when you are with Joni! And you never forget it. My daughter will never forget it. Joni does so well what every divine image bearer, every human being, has always been designed to do: sing and make melody in your heart to the Lord (see Eph. 5:19).

The book of Psalms—our Bible hymnal—teaches us to reach for lyric and melody through every journey of life. The psalms are our choirmaster but also the one singing beside us in the choir loft. They lead us, and they sing with us. The psalmist cries out, "Sing to the LORD, bless his name; tell of his salvation from day to day." Our singing to the Lord is not a blank or an escape, but wades through real life and drinks richly of Truth. Our singing to the Lord is to tell something, namely Christ's salvation. Our singing to the Lord is for more than special occasions, but to be "day to day" (Ps. 96:2).

Joni is a "day-to-day" singer to the Lord. On good days. On sick days. On loud days. On whisper days. On bright days. On dark days. Especially the dark days. The song doesn't stop. And when she has struggled to find the breath, she has been held up by those who sing with her and for her.

It is a lifeline to her. Songs of the Lord weave through her days and have been like an evergreen garland of hope around her neck.

Throughout the Bible and throughout the history of good hymnody, we see that the songs and singing of the church are essential to all of life. They are the sound of our future. They gather in and they send out. They search the soul and they lift up. They teach the word and shape our prayers. They give courage to fight and guide toward green pastures for rest. They are deep wells and high mountaintops. They are a place to bring our children.

You will meet real-life stories in these pages. Testimonies to God's faithfulness, the Lord who has been with Joni and who is with all who look to him. He is the one great Savior reaching to all of us who each day bear burdens we cannot carry.

The poet Malcolm Guite describes Psalm 1 and the deep-rooted tree that is the believer's life:

> Come to the place, where every breath is praise,
> And God is breathing through each passing breeze.
> Be planted by the waterside and raise
> Your arms with Christ beneath these rooted trees.[2]

Enjoy the rustling leaves of these pages and the forest of saints who have gone before us. May you sing with them through the darkness of the night and the breaking of the day. Come and do what we have always loved to do—sing with Joni as she sings to him.

Sing wherever you are of the hope that is leading us home.

Keith and Kristyn Getty
NORTHERN IRELAND

Before You Begin

Have you ever wondered when Jesus sang? We can be sure he did in synagogue during Shabbat or at religious festivals in Jerusalem—I can see him as a boy standing with his family in the temple court, gazing up at the Levites who led everyone in song. Certainly he was taught to sing the Hallel during Jewish Passover—every good Jewish boy sang those psalms. Singing must have come naturally to Jesus.

Did he hum a psalm when he worked in his father's carpenter shop? Surely he knew scores of hymns written by Asaph, David's choirmaster. Walking with his disciples in a stiff sea breeze along the shores of Galilee, was Jesus the one who'd first strike up a tune? Did the others chime in? What about when his heart filled with so much joy that he had to spread his arms wide and let loose with a song?

There is only one place in the Bible where it is recorded that Jesus sang. The scene is not on a sunny hillside, not at a joy-filled wedding; it is not as Jesus crossed the sea in a boat with his friends, or as he took a solitary walk up a hill in the cool of early dawn. Rather, the scene for the song was in the upper room the night he was betrayed.

Matthew 26:30 describes the moment. It happened when Jesus gave his disciples the bread and wine. After that, "when they had sung a hymn, they went out to the Mount of Olives." Of all the times and places that God chose to have us remember his Son singing, it is when he was led to his death. This was the one horrible moment—recorded for posterity—when our Savior sang. Consider the implications for us:

He was on the brink of that great depth of misery into which he was about to plunge, and yet he would have them sing a hymn. What does he teach us by it? Does he not say to each of us, his followers, "I, your Master, by my example would instruct you to sing even when the last solemn hour is come. I am your singing-master . . . in which my dying voice shall lead you: notwithstanding all the griefs which overwhelm my heart, I will play the chief musician, and be to you the sweet singer of Israel."[3]

It is no coincidence that a hymn echoed in Jesus's heart as he stared into the jaws of incomprehensible suffering. And God boldly asks us to do the same when our time of great affliction arrives. "For to this you have been called, because Christ also suffered for you, leaving you an example, so that you might follow in his steps" (1 Pet. 2:21).

My Song in Suffering

I have lived with quadriplegia for more than half a century and have wrestled with chronic pain for much of that time. I struggle with breathing problems and am in an ongoing battle against cancer. All this makes for a perfect storm for discouragement.

Yet when my hip and back are frozen in pain, or it's simply another weary day of plain paralysis, I strengthen myself with Jesus's example in the upper room. My suffering Savior has taught me to always choose a song—a song that fortifies my faith against discouragement and breathes hope into my heart. And so I daily take up my cross to the tune of a hymn.

But not just any tune or lyrics. The song must possess enough spiritual muscle to barge into my soul and shake awake a hopeful response. It must be a hymn whose lyrics raise me onto a different plane spiritually; it must summon in me the emotional wherewithal to remember my station in

life so that I can rise above my circumstances. A well-crafted song of suffering—filled with truths about life and God—has power to do that. It grinds biblical truth into our souls, like a pestle grinding powder in a crucible.

Singing songs of suffering is not an option for Christ-followers. It is not a mere invitation. When Christians in Colossae were struggling to survive under the reign of the madman Nero, Paul ordered them, "Let the word of Christ dwell in you richly . . . singing psalms and hymns and spiritual songs, with thankfulness in your hearts to God" (Col. 3:16). When the Ephesians were being persecuted and threatened with torture, Paul commanded them to encourage "one another in psalms and hymns and spiritual songs, singing and making melody to the Lord with your heart" (Eph. 5:19). Paul himself takes his own advice when—bloodied, bruised, and shackled in jail—he boisterously sings a hymn at midnight, proving that spiritual songs can provide powerful ammunition for embattled Christians! (Acts 16:25).

Life is war. I wake up every morning feeling besieged by various afflictions. Nevertheless, I see myself in the choir of Levites who marched onto the battlefield in front of Jehoshaphat's troops, singing, "Give thanks to the Lord, for his steadfast love endures forever" (2 Chron. 20:21–22).

In the morning, I tune my heart with a hymn. And at night when pain keeps me awake, when I cannot reposition myself and I don't want to bother my husband a third time, when my mind is so foggy I can barely put two sentences together in prayer, I lean on Scripture. But I also lean on stanzas of great hymns I've memorized over the years.

> All the way my Savior leads me,
> Cheers each winding path I tread;
> Gives me grace for every trial,
> Feeds me on the living Bread.
> When my weary soul may falter,
> And my soul athirst may be,
> Gushing from the Rock before me,
> Lo, a Spring of joy I see![4]

Let the Song Dwell in You Richly

Before you sing it, you must know it. And know it by heart.

My husband often brags about me to friends, saying, "Just hum a line from a 60s song; something by the Beatles or the Beach Boys—anything— and believe me, Joni will know it!" That is nothing to boast about, but Ken is fascinated that I know all these old songs by heart. Growing up with

older sisters who were glued to their transistor radios, my mind could not help but be saturated with songs by Elvis Presley or the Supremes. I unwittingly memorized scores of Top 40 hits by simply sharing a bedroom with my siblings.

There are far better anthems for our lives than frivolous songs that cater to the flesh, dull the spirit, or dig up tarnished memories and old regrets. There are courageous, celestial anthems to learn—hymns that carry us from strength to strength, from faith to faith, and from grace to grace. Brave songs that shore up our hearts for life's battles.

It is why hymns should be memorized. You've heard it said, "We are what we eat," but I say, "We are what we sing." Even now, I work hard to retrain my memory as I uproot those old pop tunes with their lyrics as worthless as cotton candy. In their place, I have hardwired my brain to default to valiant hymns. They now comprise the musical score for my life. Why give the precious real estate of my brain cells to things that weigh my spirit down rather than elevate it?

Memorizing hymns gives a head start in grasping Christian doctrine, and their melodies enrich us more than we realize. Our minds are programmed to remember patterns in music better than we remember patterns in words alone. "Every culture has songs and rhymes to help children learn the alphabet, numbers, and other lists. Even as adults, we are limited in our ability to memorize series or to hold them in mind

unless we use [musical] patterns—and the most powerful of these devices are rhyme, meter, and song."[5]

God himself used music to help his people remember his words. As Israel was about to enter the promised land, God instructed Moses in Deuteronomy 31 to teach his people a song so that they would remember not only his promises but also his dire warnings. The lesson is clear: focus on singing words that God wants you to remember.

Your Songs of Suffering

You most likely picked up this book because, first, you are suffering. Whether physically or emotionally, it hurts bad and it's hard. Second, you need a song. The music has drained from your heart, and you need bold, celestial anthems to fill the void. Songs that will help you go from strength to strength.

I want to be your song leader. The hymns in this volume are ones that I turn to when I need help in persevering through pain. I know most of them by memory, and when I sing them, even if ever so feebly, I sense the Spirit say, "Joni, this is rich stuff. Here's truth you can feed on. Here's solid doctrine you've almost forgotten in your pain. Here's inspiration to help you keep going!"

This book will have fulfilled its purpose if you learn by heart the songs in each chapter.

Also, you'll learn a devotional lesson based on each hymn. I have gleaned these lessons from either a heart-stirring event that has moved me or from a personal experience, often from my childhood. I also write about a few of my Pain Pals (precious suffering saints for whom I pray daily, friends who pick up their cross every day to the tune of a hymn).

I love all the songs I've chosen for this book. They are my companions in seasons of loneliness and my comrades when I am fighting discouragement. Their lyrics pour out consolation when my soul is weary, and they drag me back to the fold when my heart goes astray. Best of all, these hymns and spiritual songs provide rousing words of worship that are fitting for the King of the universe.

And take heart! Soon you will sing a different song of suffering. You will gladly sing it on that day when God "will wipe away every tear from their eyes, and death shall be no more, neither shall there be mourning, nor crying, nor pain anymore, for the former things have passed away" (Rev. 21:4). John Piper describes this glorious song: "We will sing about suffering through eternity—*not our suffering, but Christ's*. We will remember that he was pierced for our transgressions and crushed for our iniquities, and our hearts will overflow with a song of praise to the Lamb who endured the ultimate pain to redeem us."[6]

We will glorify our gallant Lord for choosing to sing on the night of his betrayal. We will lionize him for marching to his death with that same song reverberating in his heart. Join me in following in his steps. Turn up the wattage on the glory of your singing Savior, the man of sorrows who paved the way for you as he lifted a song before he lifted his cross.

Oh, may we do the same.

PART 1

Songs of Comfort

For God alone, O my soul, wait in silence,
for my hope is from him.
PSALM 62:5

1 Be Still My Soul

Be still, my soul! for God is on your side;
Bear patiently the cross of grief or pain:
Leave to your God to order and provide,
Who through all changes faithful will remain.
Be still, my soul! your best, your heav'nly Friend
Through thorny ways leads to a joyful end.

Be still, my soul! for God will undertake
To guide the future surely as the past.
Your hope, your confidence, let nothing shake;
All now mysterious shall be clear at last.
Be still, my soul! the waves and winds still know
The voice that calmed their fury long ago.

Be still, my soul! the hour is hast'ning on
When we shall be forever in God's peace;
When disappointment, grief, and fear are gone,
Love's joys restored, our strivings all shall cease.
Be still my soul! when change and tears are past,
All safe and blessed we shall meet at last.

—Katharina von Schlegel (1752)

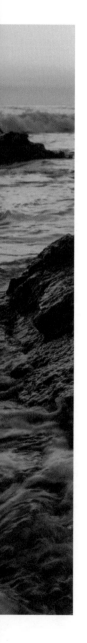

Be still my soul . . .
you are building trust in God

For God alone, O my soul, wait in silence, for my hope is from him.
—PSALM 62:5

Hedged in.

Anxious and confined. Pressed into a space so constricting that you feel like you can't even get your breath. Have you been there?

The four walls of a sick room can feel confining, and so can "sheltering in place" during the coronavirus. For most of 2020, Ken and I did okay in the restricted space of our home, but then the insidious virus somehow crept through our front door. Contracting COVID-19 felt like a death sentence for me, a quadriplegic.

With chills and a high fever, I lay flat in bed, nervous and a little fearful. The tightness and gurgling in my bronchial passages made me feel claustrophobic, for I was not able to raise myself on my elbows to cough. COVID was like an invisible hand pressing an invisible pillow over my face. It was far worse at night.

Should I go to the hospital? No, I decided, *they won't allow Ken to stay and help me.* And I was in big need of help. Friends who normally chip in were either out of town or afraid of catching my virus and spreading it to their families. For several days, we were on our own. In the dark, I couldn't bring myself to awaken my sick husband, who also contracted the bug. I lay motionless for hours, biting my lip, watching the digital clock on my ceiling, and trying to fight off suffocating panic and pain.

I felt like the prophet who wrote, "He has walled me about so that I cannot escape" (Lam. 3:7). There's a lot of lament in that verse. But there is also a lot of comfort. Do you see it? Who was the stonemason who walled in Jeremiah? Whose hedge and whose walls are we speaking about here? This is God's hedge. Those are God's walls. And at 2:00 a.m. in the dark, I knew it was God's virus. His providence permitted it to invade my body. It wasn't a random circumstance. It was God's doing. And God was on my side.

It gave me confidence to whisper-sing the same hymn that had comforted me decades earlier when I was a frightened teenager in the hospital, facing a life of paralysis:

> Be still, my soul! for God is on your side;
> Bear patiently the cross of grief or pain:
> Leave to your God to order and provide,
> Who through all changes faithful will remain.
> Be still, my soul! your best, your heav'nly Friend
> Through thorny ways leads to a joyful end.

Claustrophobia is not always about congested lungs. Sometimes circumstances wall us in so tightly that we feel like we're being crushed. Although it *feels* that way, the ironclad promise in 2 Corinthians 4:8 offers great assurance: "We are afflicted in every way, *but not crushed*." Our bodies may suffer, but God will always provide enough grace so that our souls do not suffer harm.

True, walls are cold, hard, and foreboding, and even Robert Frost wrote, "Something there is that doesn't love a wall."[7] But we can be at peace with the walls and ways of our sovereign God. He has *placed* us, not misplaced us. The love of our God is supreme and matchless, and he only confines us 'round for a wise and timely purpose. For those who believe in the

29

wisdom of a sovereign God, even a heartbreaking confinement can be a place of building trust.

As well as a place to sing.

As you sing stillness into your soul above your walls that confine, you may find that hedged-in place is the widest—and most wonderful—place to build trust in Jesus Christ.

A high hedge cannot shut out our view of the skies, nor can it prevent the soul from looking up into the face of God. Because there is so little else to see, the hedged-in Christian cannot afford to hang his head. He must look up. It is that Christian who may possibly apprehend God more fully than the disciple who moves about freely and unconfined. *

*Shannon Gallatin, Pain Pal, For more information about the Pain Pals, see the acknowledgments on p. 186.

BE STILL MY SOUL

1. Be still, my soul! for God is on your side; bear pa-tient-ly the
2. Be still, my soul! for God will un-der-take to guide the fu-ture
3. Be still, my soul! the hour is has-t'ning on when we shall be for-

cross of grief or pain. Leave to your God to or-der and pro-vide;
sure-ly as the past. Your hope, your con-fi-dence, let noth-ing shake;
-ev-er in God's peace; When dis-ap-point-ment, grief, and fear are gone,

who through all chang-es faith-ful will re-main. Be still, my soul! your
all now mys-te-rious shall be clear at last. Be still, my soul! the
love's joys re-stored, our striv-ings all shall cease. Be still, my soul! when

best, your heav'n-ly Friend through thorn-y ways leads to a joy-ful end.
waves and winds still know the voice that calmed their fu-ry long a-go.
change and tears are past, all safe and bless-ed we shall meet at last.

Words: Katharina von Schlegel, 1752; trans. Jane Borthwick, 1855, alt.
Music: Jean Sibelius, 1899

FINLANDIA
10 10 10 10 10 10

2 Jesus, Lover of My Soul

Jesus, lover of my soul,
Let me to thy bosom fly,
While the nearer waters roll,
While the tempest still is high;
Hide me, O my Savior, hide,
Till the storm of life is past;
Safe into the haven guide;
O receive my soul at last!

Other refuge have I none;
Hangs my helpless soul on thee;
Leave, ah! leave me not alone,
Still support and comfort me.
All my trust on thee is stayed,
All my help from thee I bring;
Cover my defenseless head
With the shadow of thy wing.

Plenteous grace with thee is found,
Grace to cover all my sin;
Let the healing streams abound;
Make and keep me pure within.
Thou of life the fountain art;
Freely let me take of thee;
Spring thou up within my heart,
Rise to all eternity.

—*Charles Wesley (1740)*

Jesus, lover of my soul . . .
you are my comfort in every loss

For your love is better than wine.
—SONG OF SOLOMON 1:2

Whenever talk would turn to favorite movies, my daddy would bring up the 1941 classic *How Green Was My Valley*, a romanticized view of coal mining in South Wales during the last century. No wonder he loved it. Born in 1900, he worked in his father's coal business, rising before dawn to deliver coal in a horse-drawn wagon. I grew up thinking all Welsh coal miners and their families lived idyllic lives in quaint villages.

That image dissolved one wet, foggy morning in 1966. In the hamlet of Aberfan, South Wales, the children in Pantglas Junior School were about to be dismissed for an early vacation. Beyond the street in front of the school stood an ominous ridge of coal waste that had accumulated into a small mountain. For years, town leaders had been expressing their concerns to the government about the steep, black slurry that kept mounting daily to new and more dangerous heights. The gradient was so steep that they wondered how it could possibly remain in position during heavy rains.[8]

That same wet, foggy morning, workers at the top of the mountain noticed massive chunks of coal waste beginning to crack and slip. Before they knew it, a glistening black avalanche rumbled and raced toward the village below, a tsunami of sludge sweeping past embankments, burying outlying cottages, and slamming into the school. In an instant, the chatter of schoolchildren was silenced under a weight of quicksand-like sludge.[9]

Villagers rushed to the scene with shovels and picks, desperately scraping and digging on hands and knees with cups—with anything—to free the children. But by 11:00 a.m., there were no more cries to be heard. Sobbing mingled with prayers as they frantically worked over the next 24 hours, hoping against hope. In the end, 116 students from ages seven to eleven years old lost their lives inside the sludge-entombed school.[10]

News of the Welsh tragedy raced around the world. People were shocked, especially when they learned such horror *could* have been avoided. I was sixteen years old at the time, thinking how Hollywood had duped us all about life in the shadow of coal mines.

A mass funeral for most of the children took place at a cemetery above the village. The ten thousand people who attended were cordoned off from family members who lined each side of the 80-foot-long trench. Numb with grief, parents stared at eighty-one small coffins placed in a row.[11] Sensing the historic moment, BBC journalists snapped black-and-white photos. Then something happened that sent chills.

Someone began singing "Jesus, Lover of My Soul" to the Aberystwyth tune so familiar to Welshmen: "Plenteous grace with thee is found, grace to cover all my sin; let the healing streams abound, make and keep me pure within." Soon, a chorus of hefty voices in seamless harmony were lauding the resurrected Christ. The fiercest critic dared not attribute it to stubborn Welsh stoicism—the moment was just too sacred.[12]

Geerhardus Vos said:

> If only we will take the courage to fix our gaze deliberately upon the stern countenance of grief, and enter unafraid into the darkest recesses of our trouble, we shall find the terror gone, for the Lord has been there before us, and, coming out again, has left the place transfigured, making of it by the grace of his resurrection a house of life, the very gate of heaven.[13]

It's what happened the day heaven's gates opened above Aberfan, South Wales.

Lord, be pleased to shake my clay cottage before Thou throwest it down. Make it totter awhile before it doth tumble. Let me be summoned before I am surprised. *

"20 Most Powerful Reformers Quotes," Evangelica Sola, accessed July 8, 2021, https://jonathanhayashi.com/.

JESUS, LOVER OF MY SOUL

1. Je - sus, lov - er of my soul, let me to thy bos - om fly,
2. Oth - er ref - uge have I none; hangs my help - less soul on thee;
3. Plen - teous grace with thee is found, grace to cov - er all my sin;

while the near - er wa - ters roll, while the tem - pest still is high;
leave, ah! leave me not a - lone, still sup - port and com - fort me;
let the heal - ing streams a - bound, make and keep me pure with - in.

hide me, O my Sav - ior, hide, till the storm of life is past;
all my trust on thee is stayed, all my help from thee I bring;
Thou of life the Foun - tain art; free - ly let me take of thee;

safe in - to the ha - ven guide; O re - ceive my soul at last.
cov - er my de - fense - less head with the shad - ow of thy wing.
spring Thou up with - in my heart, rise to all e - ter - ni - ty.

Words: Charles Wesley, 1740
Music: Joseph Parry, 1879

ABERYSTWYTH
77 77 D

3   Abide with Me

Abide with me: fast falls the eventide;
The darkness deepens; Lord, with me abide.
When other helpers fail and comforts flee,
Help of the helpless, O abide with me.

I need thy presence every passing hour.
What but thy grace can foil the tempter's pow'r?
Who like thyself my guide and stay can be?
Through cloud and sunshine, O abide with me.

I fear no foe with thee at hand to bless,
Ills have no weight, and tears no bitterness.
Where is death's sting? Where, grave, thy victory?
I triumph still, if thou abide with me.

Hold thou thy cross before my closing eyes.
Shine through the gloom and point me to the skies.
Heav'n's morning breaks, and earth's vain shadows flee;
In life, in death, O Lord, abide with me.

—*Henry Francis Lyte (1847)*

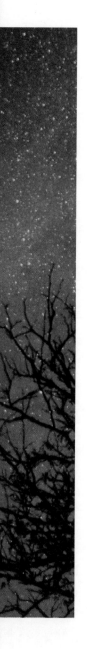

Abide with me . . .
and you will bear fruit

I am the true vine, and my Father is the vinedresser. . . .
Every branch that does bear fruit he prunes, that it may bear
more fruit. . . . Abide in me, and I in you.
—JOHN 15:1–4

I once visited an apple orchard in western Maryland at grafting time. I watched the fruit grower run his hand along the bark of a tree, take his pocketknife, and cut a slanting wound into the heart of the wood. He then wedged a freshly sliced twig into the damp interior, edge to edge. By autumn, fat crunchy apples dangled from the grafted branch.

Like an orchard grower, the Lord is always after an abundance of fruit in us, his plantings. But as John Bunyan describes, "growth in Christ is not the smooth, easy-going process some men seem to think. . . . It is wounding work, this cutting and breaking of the hearts. But without wounding there is no saving. . . . Where there is grafting of something lesser into the greater, there will always be a cutting, for the graft must be let in with a wound. To tie it on with a string would be of no use. Heart must be set to heart and edge to edge, or there will be no life; no sap from root to branch to bud and flower to fruit."[14]

God is not interested in you putting your name on the dotted line of an eternal insurance policy. He wants you heart and soul, root, bud and branch, sun and rain and soil. He wants *everything*. If in our suffering we wonder, *God, what are you doing?* the answer is straightforward: God grafts those he loves.

Pruning and cutting, grafting, and wounding are the metaphors Scripture invites us to use when describing abiding in Christ. Jesus does not say, "I am the battery docking station and you are the cell phone." Our Savior is not a wall socket into whom we plug to get our spiritual battery charged. It doesn't work that way. To abide in Christ is to be painfully grafted into "the branch of the LORD" (Isa. 4:2). And it requires the knife of suffering to make that happen.

Over five decades ago, when the reality of permanent paralysis began to settle in, the stanzas of "Abide with Me" became a refrain for my wounded heart, especially the first lines. I was frightened about the future, helpless, and so I found consolation in singing:

Abide with me: fast falls the eventide;
The darkness deepens; Lord, with me abide.
When other helpers fail and comforts flee,
Help of the helpless, O abide with me.

Although I was figuratively and literally helpless, over time I learned to rest in the branch, expecting nothing, railing at nothing, and not begrudging others when they weren't able to empathize. I didn't even mind when they drifted away. Andrew Murray explains, "[Abiding] is to have a blessed home in the Lord, where I can go in and shut the door, and kneel to my Father in secret, and am at peace as in a deep sea of calmness, when all around and above is trouble. . . . It is the fruit of the Lord Jesus Christ's redemptive work on Calvary's cross, manifested in those of His own who are definitely subject to the Holy Spirit."[15]

Are you a rigid twig stiffening against the sharp edge of suffering's knife? It may feel terribly painful, but release your anxiety. Yield to the blade.

Be wedged against Christ, heart to heart, for affliction will not permit you to be his mere acquaintance. He wants you as his most prized of disciples. And when an abundance of fruit—love, joy, peace, gentleness, and kindness—finally sweetens your suffering, you can sing this hymn as your praise to your wise and good vinedresser.

Jesus knew that we would have questions. To prepare us for them, He urged us to abide in His love. Even when God's ways are inexplicable, His love is reliable. So we remain doggedly devoted to Him.*

*Julie Ackerman Link "Dogged Devotion," *Our Daily Bread*, September 20, 2010, https://odb.org/.

ABIDE WITH ME

1. A - bide with me: fast falls the e - ven - tide;
2. I need thy pres - ence eve - ry pass - ing hour.
3. I fear no foe with thee at hand to bless,
4. Hold thou thy cross be - fore my clos - ing eyes.

the dark - ness deep - ens; Lord, with me a - bide.
What but thy grace can foil the tempt - er's pow'r?
ills have no weight, and tears no bit - ter - ness.
Shine through the gloom and point me to the skies.

When oth - er help - ers fail and com - forts flee,
Who like thy - self my guide and stay can be?
Where is death's sting? Where, grave, thy vic - to - ry?
Heav'n's morn - ing breaks, and earth's vain shad - ows flee;

Help of the help - less, O a - bide with me.
Through cloud and sun - shine, O a - bide with me.
I tri - umph still, if thou a - bide with me.
in life, in death, O Lord, a - bide with me.

Words: Henry Lyte, 1847
Music: William H. Monk, 1861

EVENTIDE
10 10 10 10

4   It Is Well with My Soul

When peace like a river attendeth my way,
When sorrows like sea billows roll;
Whatever my lot thou hast taught me to say,
"It is well, it is well with my soul!"

It is well with my soul;
It is well, it is well with my soul!

Though Satan should buffet, though trials should come,
Let this blest assurance control:
That Christ hath regarded my helpless estate,
And hath shed his own blood for my soul. [Refrain]

My sin—oh, the bliss of this glorious thought—
My sin, not in part, but the whole,
Is nailed to the cross, and I bear it no more;
Praise the Lord, praise the Lord, O my soul! [Refrain]

For me, be it Christ, be it Christ hence to live;
If dark hours about me shall roll,
No pang shall be mine, for in death as in life
Thou wilt whisper thy peace to my soul. [Refrain]

—Horatio Spafford (1876)

It is well with my soul . . .
he is enough

We are hard pressed on every side, but not crushed.
—2 CORINTHIANS 4:8 NIV

When Paul spoke of being hard-pressed on every side, he wasn't speaking lightly. He wasn't saying, "Whew, things were a little tough for a while." He was describing pain that was so oppressive that he "despaired of life itself" (2 Cor. 1:8). How in the same sentence can Paul be pressed in like that, yet not be crushed?

Nancy Severns knows the answer. She has been bedridden for five years with pain from Ehlers-Danlos syndrome, a debilitating disorder that affects her entire body, inside and out—her ribs even slip out of place! When all feels torturous, Nancy slowly inhales and calmly acknowledges the pain. She then enters it much like the three Hebrews entering Nebuchadnezzar's fiery furnace. There in the middle of hellish, white-hot agony, she finds the Son of God. And she feels his protective embrace.

I do the same thing. When the fangs of pain sink into my hips and lower back, it's a signal to begin deep breathing. I then walk into the pain and hold it near me, even have a conversation with it. I don't fret and say, "This is killing me," or, "I can't stand this," or "Oh, no, not again!" Words like that are fraught with anxiety, and we all know that fear only exacerbates the problem. Instead, like Nancy, I serenely acknowledge the pain and allow it to press me in on all sides, and then I take one more step of faith: I ask my Savior to not let it crush me, but to meet me in it. He *always* does.

This is a hard discipline learned over time. Brad Stulberg, an analyst and performance coach, explains:

> Pain can be a bit of a catch-22: often the more you try to wish it away, the worse it becomes. . . . Pain is pain, and it's bad enough. Suffering—which features distress and misery layered on top—occurs only when you try to fight that pain. . . . When you're in pain, be it physical or emotional, you need not make it worse by resisting it. It's better to accept the pain and commit to accomplishing your goals, and often that means carrying the pain with you.[16]

It takes discipline to carry pain with you while not letting it asphyxiate you. Horatio Spafford, the composer of "It Is Well with My Soul," knew how to carry his pain well. A year after he lost his son to scarlet fever, the Great Chicago Fire of 1871 destroyed all his business holdings. Spafford then decided to take his family to England, sending his wife and four daughters ahead on the SS *Ville du Havre*. While crossing the ocean, the ship sank after colliding with another vessel. His four daughters perished. Spafford's wife survived and sent him a telegram: "Saved alone." Shortly afterward, as he sailed to meet his grieving wife, he wrote "It Is Well with My Soul" as his ship passed the place where his daughters had died.[17]

How was it that a tidal wave of grief did not sweep Horatio Spafford over the rail and into the dark waters that swallowed his daughters? How is it that Nancy Severns lies in bed, stiff with pain for years, yet finds peace? Even I look in the mirror and wonder, *How is it I keep smiling after so many years of quadriplegia?*

You could experience a baker's dozen of serious issues layered one on top of another. Financial pressures. Health pressures. Relationship pressures. Spiritual warfare pressures. The pressure of unthinkable grief or cruel pain. It will not crush you if you believe Christ is *in* it. All that matters is knowing Jesus is walking in the fiery furnace with you. The pain may feel white-hot, but be encouraged—his "peace like a river" is able to quench every anxiety and fear.

When that happens, you will know—really know—how to sing "It is Well with My Soul." You will know how to be in turmoil well. How to be downcast well. How to suffer well. How to be in an unhappy place *very* well.[18]

Never run from suffering, but bear it silently, patiently, and submissively, with the assurance that it is God's way of instilling iron into your spiritual life. Your iron crown of suffering precedes your golden crown of glory, and iron is entering your soul to make it strong and brave. *

*F. B. Meyer, "Iron Saints—Streams in the Desert," Crosswalk.com, December 27, 2020, https://www.crosswalk.com/.

IT IS WELL WITH MY SOUL

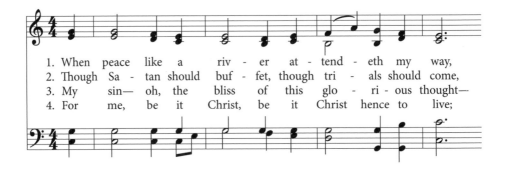

1. When peace like a riv - er at - tend - eth my way,
2. Though Sa - tan should buf - fet, though tri - als should come,
3. My sin— oh, the bliss of this glo - ri - ous thought—
4. For me, be it Christ, be it Christ hence to live;

when sor - rows like sea bil - lows roll; what - ev - er my lot,
let this blest as - sur - ance con - trol: that Christ hath re - gard -
My sin, not in part, but the whole, is nailed to the cross,
if dark hours a - bout me shall roll, no pang shall be mine,

thou hast taught me to say, "It is well, it is well
-ed my help - less es - tate, and hath shed his own blood
and I bear it no more; praise the Lord, praise the Lord,
for in death as in life thou wilt whis - per thy peace

with my soul!"
for my soul. It is well with my soul;
O my soul!
to my soul. It is well with my

soul; It is well, it is well with my soul!

Words: Horatio G. Spafford, 1876
Music: Philip P. Bliss, 1876

VILLE DU HAVRE

5   Come, Ye Disconsolate

Come, ye disconsolate, where'er ye languish;
Come to the mercy seat, fervently kneel.
Here bring your wounded hearts, here tell your anguish;
Earth has no sorrows that heaven cannot heal.

Joy of the desolate, light of the straying,
Hope of the penitent, fadeless and pure!
Here speaks the Comforter, in mercy saying,
"Earth has no sorrows that heaven cannot cure."

Here see the bread of life; see waters flowing
Forth from the throne of God, pure from above.
Come to the feast prepared; come, ever knowing
Earth has no sorrows but heaven can remove.

—*Thomas Moore (1816)*

Come, ye disconsolate . . .
there is comfort for even you

My soul refuses to be comforted.
—PSALM 77:2

Sometimes it's impossible to sing.

It happens, sooner or later, when you experience a bitter calamity. A lump where it's not expected. A child disappearing while at play. A car veering over the yellow line. A devastating diagnosis out of the blue. The slam of a door, then a loved one gone. When it occurs, it will feel bizarre, meaningless, and undeserved.

You won't perceive it as a test of faith or as the Lord's discipline. You won't view it as a blessing in disguise or as part of a wondrous plan engineered by a trustworthy God. Instead, the tragedy will attack every conviction you've ever held about the goodness of your Lord. You know him to be gracious and kind 99.99 percent of the time, but, oh, that wretched .01 percent when all appears malicious, cruel, and unjust.

It's what happened to my friend Peggy Campbell. For nearly thirty-five years she enjoyed a blissful marriage to her college sweetheart. They had it all, serving together as top executives in a national media corporation. Jon was diagnosed early on with Hodgkin's disease, but they took it in stride. It bonded them together. Jon became Peg's treasured confidant. Her soulmate. It was never just "Peggy"; it was always "Peggy and Jon." They were beautiful warriors together in his battle to stay healthy.

Then it turned into esophageal cancer. I don't need to share the details. His death was painfully slow, bewildering, and horrific. Peggy was numb with grief. And profoundly lonely, sitting by herself in their stately, spacious, and very empty home. Nothing could console her. But this gentle hymn came close. It was always a favorite of Jon's.

> Come, ye disconsolate, where'er ye languish;
> Come to the mercy seat, fervently kneel.
> Here bring your wounded hearts, here tell your anguish;
> Earth has no sorrows that heaven cannot heal.

This is a song for the utterly inconsolable—a person whose sorrow runs so deep it can only be eased by the strong arm of all three persons of the Trinity. And that's exactly how God portrays himself in 2 Thessalonians 2:16–17 (KJV): "Now our Lord Jesus Christ himself, and God, even our Father, which hath loved us, and hath given us everlasting consolation and good hope through grace, comfort your hearts, and stablish you."

Right there, Christ himself tenderly comforts Peg. The Father pours out immeasurable love on her, and all of it gently administered through the Holy Spirit. No gloom can linger long by her bed where stands the great triune God.

The waves of grief have never left Peggy, but at least now, they are more like gentle swells. She is now able to comfort others in the same way as her Lord—like him, Peg's heart is *always* attuned to the faint voices of others who hurt. Her heart is open toward the wounded. She sees herself as their empathetic advocate. Peggy may speak comfort with a tremble in her voice, or touch others with scarred hands, or serve with bruises that cannot be seen, but she still speaks, still reaches, and still serves, pouring out consolation from her own shattered jar of clay.

So should sorrow make you feel vulnerable and emotionally raw, if you feel defenseless, remember that all three persons of the Trinity are *for* you. Father, Son, and Holy Spirit are very familiar with sorrow and are ready to infuse you with all consolation, hope, and sustaining grace. It's something you can sing about *and* sleep on.

He hath spoken in the darkness,
In the secret of thy grief,
Sympathy so deep and tender,
Mighty for thy heart relief;
Speaking in thy night of sorrow
Words of comfort and of calm,
Gently on thy wounded spirit
Pouring true and healing balm. *

*Frances Ridley Havergal, "Listening in Darkness—Speaking in Light," in *The Poetical Works of Frances Ridley Havergal* (New York: Dutton, 1888), 237.

COME, YE DISCONSOLATE

1. Come, ye dis-con-so-late, wher-e'er ye lan-guish,
2. Joy of the des-o-late, light of the stray-ing,
3. Here see the bread of life, see wa-ters flow-ing

come to the mer-cy seat, fer-vent-ly kneel.
hope of the pen-i-tent, fade-less and pure!
forth from the throne of God, pure from a-bove.

Here bring your wound-ed hearts, here tell your an-guish;
Here speaks the Com-fort-er, in mer-cy say-ing,
Come to the feast pre-pared; come, ev-er know-ing

earth has no sor-rows that heav-en can-not heal.
"Earth has no sor-rows that heav-en can-not cure."
earth has no sor-rows but heav-en can re-move.

Words: Thomas Moore, 1816
Music: Gregory D. Wilbur
Music © 2008 Gregory D. Wilbur, www.greyfriarspress.com. Used by permission.

6   Wonderful Peace

Coming to Jesus, my Savior, I found
Wonderful peace, wonderful peace;
Storms in their fury may rage all around,
I have peace, sweet peace.

Peace, peace, wonderful peace,
peace, peace, glorious peace;
Since my Redeemer has ransomed my soul,
I have peace, sweet peace.

Peace like a river, so deep and so broad,
Wonderful peace, wonderful peace;
Resting my soul on the bosom of God,
I have peace, sweet peace. [Refrain]

Peace like a holy and infinite calm,
Wonderful peace, wonderful peace;
Like to the strains of an evening psalm,
I have peace, sweet peace. [Refrain]

Gone is the battle that once raged within,
Wonderful peace, wonderful peace;
Jesus has saved me and cleansed me from sin,
I have peace, sweet peace. [Refrain]

—Haldor Lillenas (1914)

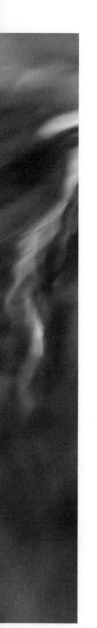

Wonderful peace . . .
it can be found in every confinement

You will keep in perfect peace him whose mind is steadfast,
because he trusts in you.
—ISAIAH 26:3 (NIV 1984)

Only after I got out of the hospital and went home was I hit with the cold facts of my paralysis. Doorways were too narrow. Sinks were too high. My knees hit the edge of the dining table. A plate of food was placed before me, but my hands were limp and useless. Someone else—at least for the first few months—had to feed me. Our cozy home felt like a prison, and I panicked. I felt nervous and trapped.

My caged feelings forced me to look at another captive. Never one to anxiously pace in a jail cell, the apostle Paul reassured his friends in Philippi, "I have learned in whatever situation I am to be content" (Phil. 4:11).

Paul was talking about a peace that gladly submits to God in all circumstances. Such quietness of heart has nothing to do with prison bars, wheelchairs, or confining situations. Instead, it bears up under *any* suffering in a satisfied and agreeable way. When the peace of Christ rules in your heart, you don't plot ways of escape, succumb to peevish thoughts, or fret needlessly. You feel at peace.

Paul learned how to live this way. "I have *learned* the secret of being content in any and every situation" (Phil. 4:12 NIV). Those situations included stoning, shipwrecks, floggings, and imprisonment. Christ's enablement was more than sufficient, and so Paul's secret was learning to lean on that fact. Learning meant making tough choices—turning *to* Christ and not away from him. Deciding this and not that. Going here and not there. Standing up to unruly emotions and seeking God's peace.

I fight every day to make choices like these. Lack of access to buildings and finding something to do with useless hands are no longer an issue for me. Neither is being fed a hamburger while others steal glances. My current issue is with pain. When pain tempts me to feel disheartened and glumly stare out a window, I stand up to my miserable emotions. I am shrewd to their cunning ways, that they could be the ruin of me. Instead, I quell those dark feelings by singing:

Peace like a river, so deep and so broad,
Wonderful peace, wonderful peace;
Resting my soul on the bosom of God,
I have peace, sweet peace.

Peace is only understood when conflicts are raging all around. Alexander Maclaren observed, "However profound and real that Divine peace is, it is to be enjoyed in the midst of warfare. God's peace is not [inertia]. The man that has it has still to wage continual conflict, and day by day to brace himself anew for the fight. The highest energy of action is the result of the deepest calm[ness] of heart. That peace of God . . . is peace militant."[19]

Christ is not a magic wand to be waved over your problems. Peace doesn't come that way. As we make the tough choices to hold fast to his grace, divine peace surges through us. As hard as life is, militant peace arrives at the instant we exercise faith during the battle. It gives us strength to say, "I can *do* this. I can make this tough choice for the honor of Christ. I can, I *will* trust him!"

So try it. Or rather, learn it. Look for peace and contentment through the hard yet simple choices you will make throughout this day. Believe God has enough grace for you, and memorize this hymn if you need a reminder. For it could be that by the time you lay your head on your pillow tonight, you will have found *his wonderful peace.*

---

*I have cast my anchor in the port of peace, knowing that present and future are in nail-pierced hands.**

*Arthur Bennett, ed., *Valley of Vision: A Collection of Puritan Prayers and Devotions* (Carlisle, PA: Banner of Truth, 1975), n.p.

WONDERFUL PEACE

1. Com - ing to Je - sus, my Sav - ior, I found won - der - ful peace,
2. Peace like a riv - er, so deep and so broad, won - der - ful peace,
3. Peace like a ho - ly and in - fi - nite calm, won - der - ful peace,
4. Gone is the bat - tle that once raged with - in, won - der - ful peace,

won - der - ful peace; storms in their fu - ry may rage all a - round,
won - der - ful peace; rest - ing my soul on the bos - om of God,
won - der - ful peace; like to the strains of an e - ven - ing psalm,
won - der - ful peace; Je - sus has saved me and cleansed me from sin,

I have peace, sweet peace. Peace, peace, won - der - ful peace,

peace, peace, glo - ri - ous peace; since my Re - deem - er has

ran - somed my soul, I have peace, sweet peace.

Words and Music: Haldor Lillenas, 1914

7 Whate'er My God Ordains Is Right

Whate'er my God ordains is right:
His holy will abideth;
I will be still, whate'er he doth,
And follow where he guideth.
He is my God; though dark my road,
He holds me that I shall not fall:
Wherefore to him I leave it all.

Whate'er my God ordains is right:
He never will deceive me;
He leads me by the proper path;
I know he will not leave me.
I take, content, what he hath sent;
His hand can turn my griefs away,
And patiently I wait his day.

Whate'er my God ordains is right:
Though now this cup, in drinking,
May bitter seem to my faint heart,
I take it, all unshrinking.
My God is true; each morn anew
Sweet comfort yet shall fill my heart,
And pain and sorrow shall depart.

Whate'er my God ordains is right:
Here shall my stand be taken;
Though sorrow, need, or
  death be mine,
Yet am I not forsaken.
My Father's care is round me there;
He holds me that I shall not fall:
And so to him I leave it all.

—*Samuel Rodigast (1675)*

Whate'er my God ordains is right . . .
his plan will never fail

Shall not the Judge of all the earth do what is just?
—GENESIS 18:25

I used to love doing jigsaw puzzles. Once, my sister knocked over the card table and sent all the pieces flying. I scrambled to recover them from under the couch, across the floor, and behind the drapes, but it was useless. The pieces had vanished, and the puzzle was ruined. It would never match the picture on the box, so I dumped the whole thing.

When there's a devastating, life-altering event, people sometimes feel as though God has kicked their table and scattered all the pieces of their lives. They long for everything to feel orderly and familiar again, so they frantically try to put their life back together as it was.

Because this feeling describes me after I broke my neck, I like to show this pencil drawing that a friend sketched after I got out of the hospital. When people observe that the image is missing many pieces, I'll explain, "It's no use trying to reconstruct your life as it once was. Trust me, you will never find what you've lost. Most of the pieces of your life will stay missing until the other side of eternity."

Ephesians 1:11 (NIV) puts the puzzle of suffering in context: "In him we were also chosen, having been

predestined according to the plan of him who works out everything in conformity with the purpose of his will." Life with its missing pieces is hidden within God's plan. When there's a botched surgery, a crippling injury, a divorce, or an unexpected death, our immediate instinct is to remake life as we once knew it. But it is beyond us.

God does not want your life to be the same as it used to be, all familiar and comfortable. He wants change. So, he resketches the picture on the cover of your puzzle box to look like his Son, Jesus, and from the pieces of your life that remain, he creates a new image that is far superior—Christ in you, the hope of glory.

You can see why "Whate'er My God Ordains Is Right" is a favorite hymn. It is filled with the satisfying doctrine of God's sovereignty as expressed in Ephesians 1:11. Samuel Rodigast composed this hymn in 1675 to comfort a sick friend.[20] Samuel wanted his disillusioned companion to grasp that he would never be content with his shattered life until he could turn to God and say, "Shall not the Judge of all the earth do right?"

> Whate'er my God ordains is right:
> His holy will abideth;
> I will be still, whate'er he doth,
> And follow where he guideth.
> He is my God; though dark my road,
> He holds me that I shall not fall:
> Wherefore to him I leave it all.

Some people think these words sound fatalistic. But do not think God's sovereignty is a defeatist "what will be, will be" way of looking at life. Dr. Ligon Duncan says, "[With determinism], it doesn't matter what you do. But the Christian deduction is always different: because God is sovereign, it *does* matter what you do!"[21]

As it concerns God's sovereign plan, your response *matters*. God invites you to play a role in redeeming your suffering by trusting him. Wisdom is not the ability to comprehend life's puzzle; it is not knowing how to make everything fit. Wisdom is trusting God when—*especially* when—all the pieces go missing. Work on *that* puzzle, and you will be in perfect conformity with the purpose of his will.

When his will for your shattered life is complete, Christ in you will be far more dazzling than you dared imagine. Far more beautiful than you ever dreamed. And far more satisfying than you ever hoped.

The strength of my hope is rooted in the confidence that God has the authority, the freedom, the wisdom, and the power to accomplish all the good he has promised to do for his embattled children. No obstacle can stop God from making all my experiences and all my brokenness serve my eternal wholeness. The main reason God's sovereignty is precious is that he has power to fulfill impossible promises to me in my seemingly hopeless condition. *

*John Piper, "When Jesus Meets Disability: How a Christian Hedonist Handles Deep Disappointment," message delivered at The Works of God Conference, November 8, 2012, Minneapolis, MN.

WHATE'ER MY GOD ORDAINS IS RIGHT

1. What-e'er my God or-dains is right: his ho-ly will a-bid-eth;
2. What-e'er my God or-dains is right: he nev-er will de-ceive me;
3. What-e'er my God or-dains is right: though now this cup, in drink-ing,
4. What-e'er my God or-dains is right: here shall my stand be tak-en;

I will be still, what-e'er he doth, and fol-low where he guid-eth.
he leads me by the prop-er path; I know he will not leave me.
may bit-ter seem to my faint heart, I take it, all un-shrink-ing.
though sor-row, need, or death be mine, yet am I not for-sak-en.

He is my God; though dark my road, he holds me that I
I take, con-tent, what he hath sent; his hand can turn my
My God is true; each morn a-new sweet com-fort yet shall
My Fa-ther's care is round me there; he holds me that I

shall not fall: where-fore to him I leave it all.
griefs a-way, and pa-tient-ly I wait his day.
fill my heart, and pain and sor-row shall de-part.
shall not fall: and so to him I leave it all.

Words: Samuel Rodigast, 1675; tr. Catherine Winkworth, 1829–1878, alt.
Music: Severus Gastorius, 1681

WAS GOTT TUT
87 87 44 88

8   Jesus, I Am Resting, Resting

Jesus! I am resting, resting
In the joy of what thou art;
I am finding out the greatness
Of thy loving heart.
Thou hast bid me gaze upon thee,
As thy beauty fills my soul,
For, by thy transforming power,
Thou hast made me whole.

Jesus, I am resting, resting,
In the joy of what thou art;
I am finding out the greatness
Of thy loving heart.

O, how great thy lovingkindness,
Vaster, broader than the sea:
O, how marvelous thy goodness,
Lavished all on me!
Yes, I rest in thee, Beloved,
Know what wealth of grace is thine,
Know thy certainty of promise,
And have made it mine. [Refrain]

Simply trusting thee, Lord Jesus,
I behold thee as thou art,
And thy love, so pure, so changeless,
Satisfies my heart;
Satisfies its deepest longings,
Meets, supplies its every need,
Compasseth me round with blessings,
Thine is love indeed. [Refrain]

Ever lift thy face upon me,
As I work and wait for thee;
Resting 'neath thy smile, Lord Jesus,
Earth's dark shadows flee.
Brightness of my Father's glory,
Sunshine of my Father's face,
Keep me ever trusting, resting,
Fill me with thy grace. [Refrain]

—*Jean Sophia Pigott (1876)*

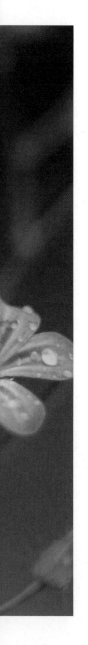

Jesus, I am resting, resting . . .
and listening too

*Return, O my soul, to your rest; for the LORD has
dealt bountifully with you.*
—PSALM 116:7

Gravity is my enemy. At least when I am in bed.

Sitting up in my wheelchair, I can breathe better, move my arms more,
and face life head-on. I can do things when I am upright, so rarely will I
ask Ken to lay me down early, even when I am in great pain. Lying in bed
means I'm more "paralyzed."

When a long illness or a pressure sore forces me into a prone position,
I may not like it, but I know it is God's doing. It is he who is making
me to lie down in green pastures (though they don't feel very green; see
Ps. 23:2). He *wants* me to lie down, and years of forced bed rest have
shown me why: "For thus said the Lord GOD, the Holy One of Israel, 'In
returning and rest you shall be saved; *in quietness and in trust shall be
your strength*'" (Isa. 30:15).

It is how "Jesus, I am Resting, Resting" became my bedroom anthem.
At night when I'm unable to breathe and am stiff with pain, when I hurt
so badly I cannot muster a prayer, my heart defaults to the stanzas of this
timeless hymn. It flows from memory: "Resting 'neath thy smile Lord
Jesus, earth's dark shadows flee." I relax into the words and am able to
make my peace with gravity—its natural downward force presses into

me like a weighted blanket as God takes gentle, firm possession of my affliction and imparts to me his *rest*.

It's totally counterintuitive for a quadriplegic like me to choose stillness, to want to stop moving, or to cease activity. But it is needed. In the same way a "rest" is needed in a piece of music. There is no audible sound during a musical rest, but it is critical to the success of a musical score. John Ruskin writes:

> During those rests we foolishly believe we have come to the end of the song. Likewise, God sends us forced leisure by allowing sickness, disappointed plans, and frustrated efforts. He brings a sudden pause in the choral hymns of our lives, and we lament that our voices must be silent. We grieve that our part is missing in the music that continually rises to the ear of our Creator. . . . [But] our part is to learn the tune and not be discouraged during the rests. . . . If we will only look up, God himself will count the time for us. With our eyes on Him, our next note will be full and clear. . . . The process is often slow and painful in this life, yet how patiently God works to teach us. And how long He waits for us to learn the lesson![22]

When I welcome forced times of rest, a calm, sweet carelessness washes over me. I can even inwardly smile and not even ask to be delivered from my restrictions. For I know when I sing this hymn, I am showing God that he's worth it. I am demonstrating to the heavenly hosts that I believe God is immensely more valuable than living life my way.

Oh, how delightful it is to "give" God that joy, to know that my trust and obedience bring him immense pleasure! And so I happily sing the chorus from my pillow: "Jesus, I am resting, resting, in the joy of what thou art; I am finding out the greatness of thy loving heart."

And I still am.

I needed the quiet so He drew me aside,
Into the shadows where we could confide.
Away from the bustle where all the day long
I hurried and worried when active and strong.

I needed the quiet tho at first I rebelled
But gently, so gently, my cross He upheld
And whispered so sweetly of spiritual things
Tho weakened in body, my spirit took wings
To heights never dreamed of when active and gay.
He loves me so greatly He drew me away.

I needed the quiet. No prison my bed,
But a beautiful valley of blessings instead—
A place to grow richer in Jesus to hide.
*I needed the quiet so He drew me aside.**

*Alice H. Mortenson's poem "I Needed the Quiet" can be found at Sallie Schaaf Borrink, A Quiet Simple Life website, accessed November 29, 2021, https://sallieborrink.com/.

JESUS, I AM RESTING, RESTING

1. Je - sus! I am rest - ing, rest - ing in the joy of what thou art;
2. O, how great thy lov - ing - kind - ness, vast - er, broad - er than the sea:
3. Sim - ply trust - ing thee, Lord Je - sus, I be - hold thee as thou art,
4. Ev - er lift thy face up - on me, as I work and wait for thee;

Refrain: Je - sus, I am rest - ing, rest - ing in the joy of what thou art;

I am find - ing out the great - ness of thy lov - ing heart.
O, how mar - vel - ous thy good - ness, lav - ished all on me!
and thy love, so pure, so change - less, sat - is - fies my heart;
rest - ing 'neath thy smile, Lord Je - sus, earth's dark shad - ows flee.
I am find - ing out the great - ness of thy lov - ing heart.

Thou hast bid me gaze up - on thee, as thy beau - ty fills my soul,
Yes, I rest in thee, Be - lov - ed, know what wealth of grace is thine,
sat - is - fies its deep - est long - ings, meets, sup - plies its eve - ry need,
Bright - ness of my Fa - ther's glo - ry, sun - shine of my Fa - ther's face,

to refrain

for, by thy trans - form - ing pow - er, thou hast made me whole.
know thy cer - tain - ty of prom - ise, and have made it mine.
com - pass - eth me round with bless - ings, thine is love in - deed.
keep me ev - er trust - ing, rest - ing, fill me with thy grace.

Words: Jean Sophia Pigott, 1876
Music: James Mountain, 1876

TRANQUILITY
87 85 D with refrain

PART 2

Songs of Strength

I love you, O Lord, my strength.
The Lord is my rock and my fortress and my deliverer,
my God, my rock, in whom I take refuge,
my shield, and the horn of my salvation, my stronghold.

PSALM 18:1–2

9 O Church, Arise

O church, arise, and put your
    armor on;
Hear the call of Christ our captain.
For now the weak can say
    that they are strong
In the strength that God has given
With shield of faith and belt of truth,
We'll stand against the devil's lies.
An army bold, whose battle cry is love,
Reaching out to those in darkness.

Our call to war, to love the
    captive soul,
But to rage against the captor;
And with the sword that makes
    the wounded whole,
We will fight with faith and valor.
When faced with trials on every side,
We know the outcome is secure.
And Christ will have the prize
    for which he died:
An inheritance of nations.

Come, see the cross, where
    love and mercy meet,
As the Son of God is stricken;
Then see his foes lie crushed
    beneath his feet,
For the Conqueror has risen!
And as the stone is rolled away,
And Christ emerges from the grave,
This victory march continues till the day
Every eye and heart shall see him.

So Spirit, come, put strength
    in every stride;
Give grace for every hurdle.
That we may run with faith
    to win the prize
Of a servant good and faithful.
As saints of old, still line the way,
Retelling triumphs of his grace,
We hear their calls, and
    hunger for the day
When with Christ we stand in glory.

—*Keith Getty and Stuart Townend (2005)*

O church, arise . . .
with the sword of the spirit in your hand

But Eleazar stood his ground and struck down the Philistines
till his hand grew tired and froze to the sword. The LORD
brought about a great victory that day.

—2 SAMUEL 23:10 (NIV)

Rika Theron lives in a dusty, seaside village on the west coast of South Africa, and although we have never met, she is one of my dearest friends. She has myalgic encephalomyelitis, an agonizing condition that has kept her housebound for over thirty-five years. "I feel as though every nerve is a damaged power cable, shooting sparks," she emailed me. "I cannot tolerate pain meds, so there is no relief. I spend roughly 90 percent of my day in my bed. I am grateful for my laptop that rests on a hospital trolley over my bed—it's my contact with the outside world."

I once told Rika about the full moon above my backyard. "I love knowing it's the same moon you can see from your bedroom window," I emailed her, to which she replied, "Oh, Joni, there's only a small window high above my bed. I haven't seen the moon in years." When I slowly reread her response, my eyes became wet and hot.

Rika is a joyous, stalwart follower of the Lord Jesus who knows her Bible inside and out. She is constantly encouraging me—and others—by posting messages filled with insightful Scriptures or essays by Charles Spurgeon, Thomas Brooks, or William Law. Although her neurological problems can cause brain fog, Rika takes advantage of clear-minded days to research and study as best she can, passing the encouragement on to others. Like me, one of her Pain Pals.

Rika finds a helpful example in Eleazar, a great warrior who stood alongside David's three mighty men. During a brutal battle against the Philistines, Israel's army gave up and fled, "but Eleazar stood his ground and struck down the Philistines till his hand grew tired and froze to the sword. The LORD brought about a great victory that day" (2 Sam. 23:10 NIV).

King David looked upon Eleazar's heroic sword grasp as proof of his bravery against a fierce enemy. David's man did not cower before the enemy; instead, he put his strength into his sword and rushed into battle with victory on his heart. He fought so hard that his hand and his sword became one.

His hand and his sword became one. This describes Rika perfectly. She clings so fiercely to the sword of the Spirit—the word of God—that it has become welded to her soul. She and the word are one. She is like David's man, encouraging me and the rest of her comrades not to succumb to enemies of fear or angst. Her Pain Pals and I look to her as though she were Eleazar himself, a warrior who never flinched from the front lines where victories for the King are won.

This Eleazar lesson is typical of the things Rika always posts. She shared this very lesson from T. De Witt Talmage, implying that we pals are in the same league as Eleazar! But we think that Talmage describes Rika: "Eleazar did not realize that the hilt of the sword was eating down into the palm of his hand, and that while he was taking hold of the sword, the sword was taking hold of him."[23]

I want my suffering to mature me as it has Rika. And so I will sing from my bed, as she does from hers. Will you do the same? I urge you to arise, put your armor on, hear the call of Christ your captain, and join us on the front lines of *your* affliction.

You march in the midst of gallant spirits, your fellow soldiers, every one the son of a Prince. . . . Every exploit of your faith . . . causes a shout in heaven, while you valiantly lay low temptations, scale difficulties, and regain ground you had lost, out of your enemies' hands. . . . Your dear Saviour stands by with a reserve for your relief. His very heart leaps for joy, to see the proof of your zeal for him in all your combats. He will not forget all the faithful service you have done in his wars on earth; but when you return out of the field, he will receive you with the same joy as he was given from his father at his return to heaven."*

*William Gurnall, *The Christian in Complete Armour*, 1662, accessed November 29, 2021, https://www.ccel.org/.

O CHURCH, ARISE

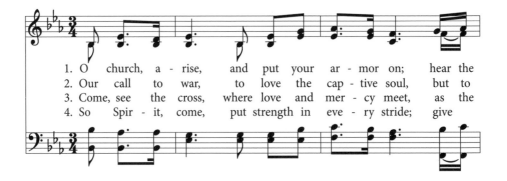

1. O church, a - rise,   and put your ar - mor on;   hear the
2. Our call   to war,   to love the cap - tive soul, but to
3. Come, see the cross, where love and mer - cy meet, as the
4. So Spir - it, come,   put strength in eve - ry stride; give

call of Christ our cap - tain. For now the weak can say that
rage a - gainst the cap - tor; and with the sword that makes the
Son of God is strick - en; then see his foes lie crushed be -
grace for eve - ry hur - dle. That we may run with faith to

they are strong in the strength that God has giv - en. With shield of
wound-ed whole, we will fight with faith and val - or. When faced with
-neath his feet, for the Con-quer - or has ris - en! And as the
win the prize of a ser - vant good and faith - ful. As saints of

faith and belt of truth, we'll stand a - gainst the dev - il's lies. An ar - my
trials on eve - ry side, we know the out - come is se - cure, and Christ will
stone is rolled a - way, and Christ e - merg - es from the grave, this vic - t'ry
old still line the way, re - tell-ing tri - umphs of his grace, we hear their

bold, whose bat - tle cry is love, reach-ing out to those in dark - ness.
have the prize for which he died: an in - her - i - tance of na - tions.
march con - tin - ues till the day eve - ry eye and heart shall see him.
calls, and hun-ger for the day when with Christ we stand in glo - ry!

Words and Music: Keith Getty and Stuart Townend

10 Immortal, Invisible, God Only Wise

Immortal, invisible, God only wise,
In light inaccessible hid from our eyes,
Most blessed, most glorious, the Ancient of Days,
Almighty, victorious, thy great name we praise.

Unresting, unhasting, and silent as light,
Nor wanting, nor wasting, thou rulest in might;
Thy justice like mountains high soaring above
Thy clouds, which are fountains of goodness and love.

To all, life thou givest, to both great and small;
In all life thou livest, the true life of all.
We blossom and flourish as leaves on the tree,
And wither and perish, but naught changeth thee.

Great Father of glory, pure Father of light,
Thine angels adore thee, all veiling their sight.
All laud we would render; O help us to see:
'Tis only the splendor of light hideth thee.

—*Walter C. Smith (1867)*

Immortal, invisible, God only wise . . .
wake me up!

To the King of the ages, immortal, invisible, the only God, be honor and glory forever and ever. Amen.
—1 TIMOTHY 1:17

I was a restless, adventurous nine-year-old in 1958, sailing with my mother and grandmother on a steamliner to Bermuda. The first morning, we awoke to threatening, gray skies somewhere off the coast of the Carolinas. I peered through the porthole, mesmerized by heaving white-capped waves.

A bitter wind and spitting rain kept most of the passengers indoors, sipping tea. Some strolled through the ship's galleries rather than brave a brisk walk on the promenade deck. My mother gathered my grandmother and me into the auditorium to watch a slide presentation about ocean currents and trade winds.

Sitting in a dark, warm room with the steady click-clicking of the projector made me restless. Why learn about ocean currents inside a stuffy room? Why weren't we out on the deck holding onto the railing with our faces to the wind and spray? Why experience the ocean secondhand?

After the slide show, and sometime before late-afternoon darkness descended, my mother conceded to my pleadings to take me outside. We bundled up and stepped through the double doors into a windy blast that flattened our hair. We waited for the seawater to recede from the deck, then made a dash for the railing. For the few minutes we held fast to the rail, we were awestruck by the thunderous beauty of the ocean. This was danger. Adventure. The highlight of the whole trip. Better than Bermuda.

Our worship of God should be like that. When it comes to worship, the Spirit longs to ignite a passionate response in us, like the child who stands facing the storm, eyes stinging and voice straining, "This is *awesome!*" But we creatures of comfort prefer paths of least resistance, and so our amazement with the Almighty often loses its edge. Comfort is a God-sedative. It numbs us to the heart-stopping, raw truth of how mighty and majestic our Savior is. Comfort drugs us into a soul slumber.

To jar us out of our spiritual sleep, God wakes us up with ice-cold splashes of suffering in the face. God intrudes on our comfortable status quo with every pain that either stabs our heart or our lower back. Like a parent who firmly presses his hands on either side of a child's face, insisting, "Look *this* way," pain turns our face toward the bracing, raw truth of who God is. If we want to worship "in spirit and truth," suffering will lead us away from a stuffy indoor approach to God and into scriptures that open the windows to real experiences of his graces (John 4:23).[24]

When affliction so muddles my thinking that I can barely put together two sentences in a prayer, I turn to the rich stanzas of "Immortal, Invisible, God Only Wise." It provides a wealthy vocabulary for worship, especially through the weary watches of the night.

I invite you to do the same. You must not allow affliction to choke out your childlike wonder of God. View your pain as a path to deeper worship, for Jesus has given you capacities for heart-shaking praise that you can scarcely imagine, even as you are in physical distress. Let God awaken those capacities. Open your eyes to Christ's power and beauty through the lens of your pain.

Then hold onto the railing—you just might be blown away in worship.

Suppose you were exploring an unknown glacier in the north of Greenland in the dead of winter. Just as you reach a sheer cliff with a spectacular view of miles and miles of jagged ice and snow mountains, a terrible storm breaks in. The wind is so strong that the fear rises that it might blow you and your party right over the cliff. But in the midst of it you discover a cleft in the ice where you can hide. Here you feel secure, but the awesome might of the storm rages on and you watch it with a kind of trembling pleasure as it surges out across the distant glaciers. At first, there was the fear that this terrible storm and awesome terrain might claim your life. But then you found a refuge and gained the hope that you would be safe. But not everything in the feeling called fear vanished. Only the life-threatening part. There remained the trembling, the awe, the wonder, the feeling that you would never want to tangle with such a storm or be the adversary of such a power. God's . . . power is behind the unendurable cold of arctic storms. Yet he cups his hand around us and says, "Take refuge in my love and let the terrors of my power become the awesome fireworks of your happy night sky."*

*John Piper, "The Pleasure of God in Those Who Hope in His Love," Desiring God, modified March 15, 1987, https://www.desiringgod.org/.

IMMORTAL, INVISIBLE, GOD ONLY WISE

1. Im - mor - tal, in - vis - i - ble, God on - ly wise, in light in - ac -
2. Un - rest - ing, un - hast - ing, and si - lent as light, nor want - ing, nor
3. To all, life thou giv - est, to both great and small; in all life thou
4. Great Fa - ther of glo - ry, pure Fa - ther of light, thine an - gels a -

-ces - si - ble hid from our eyes, most bless - ed, most glo - rious, the
wast - ing, thou rul - est in might; thy jus - tice like moun - tains high
liv - est, the true life of all. We blos - som and flour - ish as
-dore thee, all veil - ing their sight. All laud we would ren - der; O

An - cient of Days, Al - might - y, vic - to - rious, thy great name we praise.
soar - ing a - bove thy clouds, which are foun - tains of good - ness and love.
leaves on the tree, and with - er and per - ish, but naught chang - eth thee.
help us to see: 'tis on - ly the splen - dor of light hid - eth thee.

Words: Walter C. Smith, 1867
Music: Welsh melody, 18th cent.

ST. DENIO
11 11 11 11

11   Dear Refuge of My Weary Soul

Dear refuge of my weary soul,
On thee, when sorrows rise,
On thee, when waves of trouble roll,
My fainting hope relies.
To thee I tell each rising grief,
For thou alone canst heal;
Thy Word can bring a sweet relief
For every pain I feel.

Hast thou not bid me seek thy face,
And shall I seek in vain?
And can the ear of sovereign grace
Be deaf when I complain?
No, still the ear of sovereign grace
Attends the mourner's prayer;
O may I ever find access
To breathe my sorrows there.

But oh! When gloomy doubts prevail,
I fear to call thee mine;
The springs of comfort seem to fail,
And all my hopes decline.
Yet, gracious God, where shall I flee?
Thou art my only trust;
And still my soul would cleave to thee
Though prostrate in the dust.

Thy mercy seat is open still,
Here let my soul retreat;
With humble hope attend thy will,
And wait beneath thy feet.
Thy mercy seat is open still,
Here let my soul retreat;
With humble hope attend thy will,
And wait beneath thy feet.

—*Anne Steele (1760)*

Dear refuge of my weary soul . . .
your will is terrible and wonderful

God is our refuge and strength, a very present help in trouble.
—PSALM 46:1

Anne Steele weathered many of the common calamities that made life so difficult in the eighteenth century. The eldest daughter of a village pastor, she was frail and acquainted with sorrow. She lost her mother as a child and suffered a painful, debilitating injury at age nineteen. She endured the fatigue of recurring malaria. And the man she loved and hoped to marry drowned.[25]

Rather than make her sour and somber, Anne's miseries became the fertile soil for a sweeter devotion to her Savior, which, in turn, blossomed into hundreds of poems and hymns. Anne came to think of Jesus as her "bleeding, dying Lord,"[26] and she wrote about his physical afflictions in many of her 144 hymns.

Anne was not only a keen observer of Christ, but his imitator. She carried her many crosses in the same manner as he carried his. She was fascinated by the joy of Jesus, winsomely displayed in his willingness to sacrifice comfort, all for the love of serving his Father. In the same way, Anne Steele bore her grief and intractable pain as a way of serving her God. Affliction became the ministry through which she glorified her Savior. Hers was a ministry of suffering, and in 1737, at the age of twenty-one, Anne composed these words:

Dear refuge of my weary soul,
On thee, when sorrows rise,
On thee, when waves of trouble roll,
My fainting hope relies.
To thee I tell each rising grief,
For thou alone canst heal;
Thy Word can bring a sweet relief
For every pain I feel.

More than 275 years later, Sandra McCracken sang these enduring words at a conference I was attending. As I listened to her accompany herself on the piano, I sat in the audience, squirming with a painful hip. Sandra's gentle rendition of this hymn washed over me, releasing a flood of tears that seemed to drain away all my misery. Every stanza struck my soul like a tuning fork. Anne Steele, the bygone saint from the eighteenth century, was still ministering through her suffering.

There are countless suffering servants following in the steps of Anne. Like the lowly hymnwriter, they are lifelong sufferers who bear their pain as a service to God. In the spirit of Ephesians 5:1–2, they mimic their suffering Savior: "Be imitators of God, as beloved children. And walk in love, as Christ loved us and gave himself up for us, a fragrant offering and sacrifice to God."

Do you serve God in your suffering? We serve him when we imitate Jesus's endurance in our suffering. Or his patience in the face of disappointment or his perseverance while shouldering our cross. We imitate his kindness when we forget our own hardships in order to lift the spirits of others. And when we choose contentment over complaining, we imitate his glad willingness to submit to the Father's terrible yet wonderful will. All of it comprises a fragrant, sacrificial service to God.

God entrusted Anne Steele with affliction. He knew that with his grace, she would make it a ministry of suffering. God may be calling you to do the same, and, if so, you are in a hymnwriter's league. As well as the apostle Paul's, who said of his own suffering: "I thank Christ Jesus our Lord, who has given me strength, that *he considered me trustworthy, appointing me to his service*" (1 Tim. 1:12 NIV).

Join the apostle. Join Anne and others like her. There is no more beautiful service to God than to imitate Christ in your afflictions. And then to sing about it.

There are none so tender as those who have been skinned themselves. Those who have been in the chamber of affliction know how to comfort those who are there. Do not believe that any man will become a physician unless he walks the hospitals; and I am sure that no one will become a divine, or become a comforter, unless he lies in the hospital as well as walks through it, and has to suffer himself. *

*Charles Spurgeon, "The Christian's Heaviness and Rejoicing," November 7, 1858, The Spurgeon Center, https://www.spurgeon.org/.

DEAR REFUGE OF MY WEARY SOUL

1. Dear ref - uge of my wea - ry soul, on thee, when sor - rows rise,
2. But oh! When gloom - y doubts pre - vail, I fear to call thee mine;
3. Hast thou not bid me seek thy face, and shall I seek in vain?
4. Thy mer - cy seat is o - pen still, here let my soul re - treat;

on thee, when waves of trou - ble roll, my faint - ing hope re - lies.
the springs of com - fort seem to fail, and all my hopes de - cline.
And can the ear of sov - 'reign grace be deaf when I com - plain?
with hum - ble hope at - tend thy will, and wait be - neath thy feet.

To thee I tell each ris - ing grief, for thou a - lone canst heal;
Yet, gra - cious God, where shall I flee? Thou art my on - ly trust;
No, still the ear of sov - 'reign grace at - tends the mourn - er's prayer;
Thy mer - cy seat is o - pen still, here let my soul re - treat;

thy word can bring a sweet re - lief for eve - ry pain I feel.
and still my soul would cleave to thee though pros - trate in the dust.
O may I ev - er find ac - cess to breathe my sor - rows there.
with hum - ble hope at - tend thy will, and wait be - neath thy feet.

Words: Anne Steele, 1760; Music: Matt Merker

12   Were You There
(When They Crucified My Lord)?

Were you there when they crucified my Lord?
Were you there when they crucified my Lord?
Oh, sometimes it causes me to tremble, tremble, tremble.
Were you there when they crucified my Lord?

Were you there when they nailed him to the tree?
Were you there when they nailed him to the tree?
Oh, sometimes it causes me to tremble, tremble, tremble.
Were you there when they nailed him to the tree?

Were you there when they laid him in the tomb?
Were you there when they laid him in the tomb?
Oh, sometimes it causes me to tremble, tremble, tremble.
Were you there when they laid him in the tomb?

Were you there when God raised him from the tomb?
Were you there when God raised him from the tomb?
Oh, sometimes it causes me to tremble, tremble, tremble.
Were you there when God raised him from the tomb?

—*African-American Spiritual*

Were you there (when they crucified my Lord)? . . . *yes, if you claim him as Savior*

So if the Son sets you free, you will be free indeed.
—JOHN 8:36

Billy's people were poor. He was born in a sharecropper's cabin on the corner of the Jimmy Lynch farm that had no heat, no running water, and no electricity. His daddy worked hard in the fields, and it was a good day when Willie finally earned enough to move his family into a house in Texarkana. They still couldn't afford to install gas and water, but it was home sweet home.

Willie worked at the town sawmill, while Mama Teal—that's what everyone called Billy's mother—made ends meet by squeezing in domestic work at the homes of white folks. When harvesting time rolled around, she took her children to help pick cotton.

Early each morning, the truck would stop at the edge of the field and unload the workers who would get their sacks from the field boss. They would spread out and begin picking, walking, stooping, and stretching, row after row. Little Billy worked eight to ten hours a day to fill his sack. He scrambled to keep up with the older men who earned more; he knew his fifty cents a day was needed.

Billy's childhood ended one summer afternoon in 1958. The air was hot and hissing with bugs, and he was bending over and chopping—a process that thinned the cotton plants. He stood to stretch his tired back and shield his eyes. Through waves of heat, he saw his elders shimmering in the distance like ghosts. A thought seized him, *Oh, Lord, is this how my life is supposed to be?* The next instant, he heard King Davis, the burly field boss, shout, "Get back to work, boy!" The twelve-year-old went home that day feeling old.

Nearly one hundred years had passed since the Emancipation Act; even so, this little boy was feeling the weight of being a descendant of slaves. Yet there was no bitterness, for something else had been handed down from his ancestors: a love for Jesus Christ. It is why Billy's family knew so many hymns, including African-American spirituals.

Back in the seventeenth century, families of slaves were fascinated by biblical stories that paralleled their own hardships, and they created spirituals that retold those stories. Spirituals were a slave's way of expressing love for Jesus, a greater deliverer than anyone even in the abolitionist movement. It's what makes African-American spirituals unique—they can be appreciated only in the context of suffering.

Mama Teal would sing while bending over her washboard in the backyard. Sometimes it was "Were You There (When They Crucified My Lord)?" This humble and lowly woman identified with the suffering of Jesus so closely that she sung about it as though she could hear the nails tearing through her Savior's hands. Jesus was her cosuffering friend.

Although his east Texas childhood is now a distant memory, Billy Burnett still knows those old songs. When he served with distinction as Joni and Friends' chief financial officer, I would sometimes hear him hum a few in the hallways.

He is now retired, but Billy is singing more than ever. He *has* to. My friend wrestles with oppressive back pain. But like his mother, he is still smiling and singing about his cosuffering friend. This tall, kind, black man was indeed there when they crucified his Lord—he was there in the mind and the heart of his bleeding Savior, all his sins nailed to the tree with Christ.

Billy is now handing down something precious to *his* descendants—the song of the suffering servant Jesus, the only deliverer who has the power to free the humble from slavery to sin, as well as from bondage to affliction.

Yes, there are many crosses, and every one of them is heavy and painful. And it is unlikely that I would seek out even one of them on my own. Yet Jesus is never as near to me as when I lift my cross, lay it submissively on my shoulder, and welcome it with a patient and uncomplaining spirit.*

*Alexander Smellie, "Carry Your Cross," *Streams in the Desert*, Crosswalk.com, September 14, 2021, https://www.crosswalk.com/.

WERE YOU THERE
(WHEN THEY CRUCIFIED MY LORD)?

1. Were you there when they cru-ci-fied my Lord? Were you
2. Were you there when they nailed him to the tree? Were you
3. Were you there when they laid him in the tomb? Were you
4. Were you there when God raised him from the tomb? Were you

there when they cru-ci-fied my Lord?
there when they nailed him to the tree? Oh!_____
there when they laid him in the tomb?
there when God raised him from the tomb?

Some-times it caus-es me to trem-ble, trem-ble, trem-ble.

Were you there when they cru-ci-fied my Lord?
Were you there when they nailed him to the tree?
Were you there when they laid him in the tomb?
Were you there when God raised him from the tomb?

Words: African-American Spiritual
Music: adapted by John W. Work, Jr.

13   Stricken, Smitten, and Afflicted

Stricken, smitten and afflicted,
See him dying on the tree!
'Tis the Christ, by man rejected;
Yes, my soul, 'tis he, 'tis he!
'Tis the long-expected Prophet,
David's Son, yet David's Lord;
By his Son God now has spoken:
'Tis the true and faithful Word.

Tell me, ye who hear him groaning,
Was there ever grief like his?
Friends thro' fear his
   cause disowning,
Foes insulting his distress;
Many hands were raised
   to wound him,
None would interpose to save;
But the deepest stroke
   that pierced him
Was the stroke that Justice gave.

Ye who think of sin but lightly,
Nor suppose the evil great,
Here may view its nature rightly,
Here its guilt may estimate.
Mark the sacrifice appointed,
See who bears the awful load!
'Tis the Word, the Lord's Anointed,
Son of Man and Son of God.

Here we have a firm foundation,
Here the refuge of the lost;
Christ's the Rock of our salvation,
His the name of which we boast.
Lamb of God, for sinners wounded,
Sacrifice to cancel guilt!
None shall ever be confounded
Who on him their hope have built.

—*Thomas Kelly (1804)*

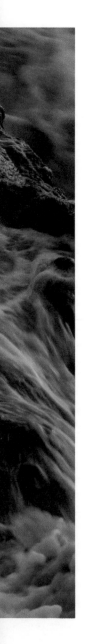

Stricken, smitten, and afflicted . . .
for you and me

Surely he has borne our griefs and carried our sorrows;
yet we esteemed him stricken, smitten by God, and afflicted.
—ISAIAH 53:4

As I write, I am sitting by our sliding glass door and admiring a woody shrub filled with tiny blossoms on our patio. *Euphorbia milii* is commonly known as "crown of thorns," and, from my vantage, I can admire its delicate flowers—brilliant with red color—and its slender spines filled with thick, nail-like thorns. Tradition says this was the bush from which the soldiers cruelly fashioned the crown they crushed into the brow of Jesus. Whether or not it's true, the "Christ-thorn," as it's also called, is a disturbing reminder of the pain our Savior endured on our behalf.

His physical torture was a mere warm-up to the real dread he faced. As he hung on the cross, Jesus began to feel a foreign sensation. Somewhere during those hours that his body was impaled, a foul odor must have wafted, not around his nose, but in his heart. He felt dirty. Human wickedness began to crawl upon his spotless being. It was the living excrement from our souls. The apple of the Father's eye began to turn brown with the rot of our sin.

From heaven, the Father must have roused himself like a lion disturbed, shaking his mane, and rising to roar against the shriveling remnant of a man hanging on the cross. Never had the Son seen the Father look at him so, never had he felt even a hint of his hot breath. It was the wrath of God being poured out like hot oil on the wounded heart of the Son of Man. The Father watched as his heart's treasure, the mirror image of himself, sank drowning into raw, liquid sin. God's stored-up rage against humankind exploded in a single direction—on the hill of Golgotha on that Friday afternoon when Jesus was crucified.[27]

It's hard to think that God offered not a drop of mercy. But Deuteronomy 21:23 gives the pitiless truth: "A hanged man [on a tree] is cursed by God."

No wonder I prize the little shrub on our patio with its pretty flowers hiding their rusted-steel thorns. And I treasure this hymn, "Stricken, Smitten, and Afflicted." I cannot sing it without casting myself upon Christ when I am in my worst discomfort. I dare not allow my hungry flesh to enjoy the worldly candy of complaining, especially since my Savior bore the wrath of hell so that I might have a home in heaven.

Pain can push you to the extremes, but I dare not allow the serpent of complaining and resentment to coil itself around my heart. I'm savvy to that snake, for I know he will choke every bit of gratitude out of me. God help me pry off his fangs! Why would I grumble against the Lord of grace when it is his very grace I desperately need to persevere and endure?

This hymn is my steady refrain through afflictions. Its words erase all lighthearted fondness or casual sentimentality about the bloody and beautiful cross. I take it seriously. God knows, when I am driven to bed in intense pain, I need his rugged and robust grace; I need his power to sustain me.

And praise the Lord that the blood sacrifice of my smitten and afflicted Savior has purchased it all (1 Cor. 1:18).

*As soon as anything presents itself to your mind as a suffering, and you feel a repugnance to it, resign yourself immediately to God with respect to it; give yourself up to Him in sacrifice, and you will find that, when the cross arrives, it will not be so very burdensome, because you had disposed yourself to a willing reception of it.**

*Jeanne-Marie Guyon, *Knowing God: Meat from the Mystics Daily Readings*, ed. J. Scott Husted, Mary Wilder Tileston (Morrisville, NC: Lulu, 2011), 279.

STRICKEN, SMITTEN, AND AFFLICTED

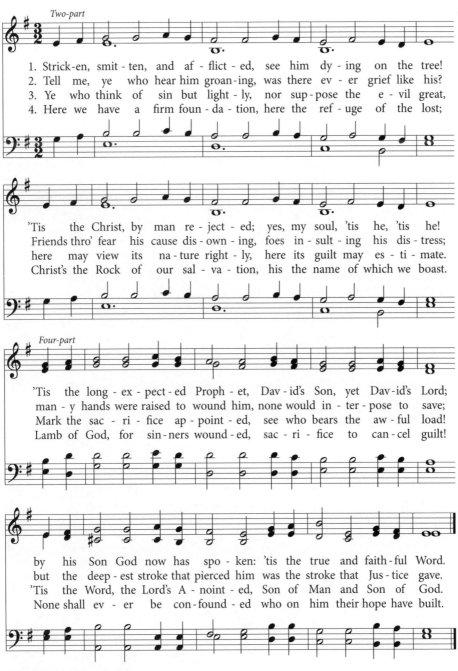

1. Strick-en, smit-ten, and af-flict-ed, see him dy-ing on the tree!
2. Tell me, ye who hear him groan-ing, was there ev-er grief like his?
3. Ye who think of sin but light-ly, nor sup-pose the e-vil great,
4. Here we have a firm foun-da-tion, here the ref-uge of the lost;

'Tis the Christ, by man re-ject-ed; yes, my soul, 'tis he, 'tis he!
Friends thro' fear his cause dis-own-ing, foes in-sult-ing his dis-tress;
here may view its na-ture right-ly, here its guilt may es-ti-mate.
Christ's the Rock of our sal-va-tion, his the name of which we boast.

'Tis the long-ex-pect-ed Proph-et, Dav-id's Son, yet Dav-id's Lord;
man-y hands were raised to wound him, none would in-ter-pose to save;
Mark the sac-ri-fice ap-point-ed, see who bears the aw-ful load!
Lamb of God, for sin-ners wound-ed, sac-ri-fice to can-cel guilt!

by his Son God now has spo-ken: 'tis the true and faith-ful Word.
but the deep-est stroke that pierced him was the stroke that Jus-tice gave.
'Tis the Word, the Lord's A-noint-ed, Son of Man and Son of God.
None shall ev-er be con-found-ed who on him their hope have built.

Words: Thomas Kelly, 1804, alt.
Music: *Geistliche Volkslieder*, 1850

O MEIN JESU, ICH MUSS STERBEN
87 87 D

14   When I Survey the Wondrous Cross

When I survey the wondrous cross
On which the Prince of glory died,
My richest gain I count but loss,
And pour contempt on all my pride.

Forbid it, Lord, that I should boast,
Save in the death of Christ, my God!
All the vain things that charm me most,
I sacrifice them to his blood.

See, from his head, his hands, his feet,
Sorrow and love flow mingled down.
Did e'er such love and sorrow meet,
Or thorns compose so rich a crown?

Were the whole realm of nature mine,
That were a present far too small.
Love so amazing, so divine,
Demands my soul, my life, my all.

—*Isaac Watts (1707)*

When I survey the wondrous cross . . .
I find strength to carry my own

For the word of the cross . . . is the power of God.
—1 CORINTHIANS 1:18

The Christian life can seem so impossible. Jesus tells us to take up our cross and follow him, but we are often clueless as to how to do it. We know Jesus doesn't want us to stiffly resign ourselves to the weight of our cross or resentfully submit to the inconvenience of it. Or to cope with it or comply with a woe-is-me attitude. Even dry acceptance of one's cross somehow seems less than what Jesus had in mind.

How we take up our cross depends largely on how we view Jesus's cross.

Jesus secured many things for us at Calvary, but resurrection power is perhaps the greatest and most life-transforming benefit. Especially when we suffer. The apostle Paul wrote that he longed to "know [Christ] and the power of his resurrection, . . . [sharing] his sufferings, becoming like him in his death" (Phil. 3:10). Resurrection power—that same mighty strength that raised Christ from the dead—is what is needed to bear a cross.[28] His mighty strength even enables us to do the unthinkable: sing sweetly under its weight.

The cross—whether yours or Christ's—is all about crucifying sin. To take up your cross means to die *to* the sins that Jesus died *for* on his cross. You don't do that by resigning yourself or by submitting, yielding, coping, or complying. It's not dryly accepting your burden. Rather, when you die to sin, you put to death *everything*. You die to comparing your lot in life with others who seem to have it easier. When you die to whining or constantly chafing against your afflictions, God strengthens you with his resurrection power, enabling you to miraculously prefer Christ over comfort, the Lord over leisure, and even embrace the Redeemer when there is no relief from pain. Only the power of the resurrection enables you to lift your cross with grace.

"When I Survey the Wondrous Cross" is so fitting here. It is the song that helps you to "pour contempt on all [your] pride." It is the song of the sufferer who agrees his cross is not one ounce too heavy, nor one inch too long.[29] It is the melody of a sufferer who will gladly go through hell and high water to be transformed like his Savior; one who refuses to coddle any sin that impaled his Lord. You feel no irksome itchiness to get out from underneath the cross God has assigned you. Even when it bites into your sanity and feels impossibly heavy, God pours out power to do the impossible. So you fall to your knees as you sing from your heart:

> When I survey the wondrous cross
> On which the Prince of glory died,
> My richest gain I count but loss,
> And pour contempt on all my pride.

When suffering nearly decimates you, when all looks dark and you wonder why you "signed up" for the Christian life in the first place—when grief numbs your soul and bitterness or despair foment in your heart—do not give up. Survey what Jesus did on his cross for you: at the cost of his own blood, he purchased the mighty strength of the resurrection for your impossible situation. And if God calls you into a deeper affliction, he will provide a deeper portion of Christ and his power.

That is worth singing about. To take up your cross God's way is to live by dying, grow by diminishing, receive by giving, and gain by losing. Just what do you gain? More joy and delight, more peace and power than you can contain.

It's what makes the cross so *wondrous*.

---

*They nailed him to a tree, not knowing that by that very act they were bringing the world to his feet. They gave him a cross, not guessing that he would make it a throne. . . . They thought they had God with his back to the wall, pinned and helpless and defeated; they did not know that it was God himself who had tracked them down. He did not conquer in spite of the dark mystery of evil. He conquered through it."**

*James Stewart, *Jesus* (Torrance, MA: Rose, 2009), 13.

WHEN I SURVEY THE WONDROUS CROSS

1. When I sur - vey the won - drous cross on which the
2. For - bid it, Lord, that I should boast, save in the
3. See, from his head, his hands, his feet, sor - row and
4. Were the whole realm of na - ture mine, that were a

Prince of glo - ry died, my rich - est gain I
death of Christ, my God! All the vain things that
love flow min - gled down. Did e'er such love and
pre - sent far too small. Love so a - maz - ing,

count but loss, and pour con - tempt on all my pride.
charm me most, I sac - ri - fice them to his blood.
sor - row meet, or thorns com - pose so rich a crown?
so di - vine, de - mands my soul, my life, my all.

Words: Isaac Watts, 1707
Music: Lowell Mason, 1825

HAMBURG
LM

15   O Sacred Head, Now Wounded

O sacred Head, now wounded,
With grief and shame weighed down,
Now scornfully surrounded
With thorns, thine only crown!
O sacred Head, what glory,
What bliss till now was thine!
Yet, though despised and gory,
I joy to call thee mine.

What thou, my Lord, hast suffered
Was all for sinners' gain.
Mine, mine was the transgression,
But thine the deadly pain.
Lo, here I fall, my Savior!
'Tis I deserve thy place.
Look on me with thy favor,
And grant to me thy grace.

What language shall I borrow
To thank thee, dearest Friend,
For this, thy dying sorrow,
Thy pity without end?
Oh, make me thine forever,
And should I fainting be,
Lord, let me never, never
Outlive my love to thee.

—Bernard of Clairvaux (1090–1153)

O sacred head, now wounded . . .
how precious you are to me

*And they clothed him in a purple cloak, and twisting together
a crown of thorns, they put it on him.*
—MARK 15:17

When you are hurting badly, you want assurance that Jesus feels your
pain. That he understands; that he's with you in it. It's why we are drawn
to hymns that extol Christ as the one who identifies with our hardships.
We sing these hymns and think, *Ah, Jesus understands me. He realizes what
I'm going through. He's been tested as I have. He resonates with my suffering.*

"O Sacred Head, Now Wounded" is not like that.

This traditional Good Friday hymn forces us to identify with Jesus in
his suffering and—if it were possible—helps us to understand what *he*
went through. Written in a mournful minor key with a slow and majestic
meter, each heartbreaking stanza pries your attention off of your own
wounds and onto Christ's.

I admire sufferers who are masters at this. Keeping exquisite focus on
Christ and his cross—rather than theirs—they make less of themselves
and more of Jesus. Like my friend Barbara Brand.

Years ago she was diagnosed with multiple sclerosis and lesions in her
brain. The MS was a hard enough pill to swallow, but the lesions were
worse, creating constant, excruciating head trauma. In the beginning,
she was unable to speak, smile, or even gesture. Even breathing would

ignite nausea and uncontrollable pain. To this day, Barbara is, for the most part, bedridden.

"Today I received forty-one injections into my skull and neck," she recently emailed me. And then she told me:

It's a regular procedure, and whenever the needles sink deep into my head, the extreme pain brings into sharp focus Jesus and his crown of thorns. The image calms my heart, but best of all, it binds me to his love. I picture my Savior yielding to the spike-like barbs, wholly embracing his own suffering to rescue me. So, when needles plunge into my skull, my heart is cheered knowing that he is beckoning me into a deeper sanctum of sharing in his sufferings. Wonder of wonders, in some small measure, lowly me gets to identify with and enter *his* grief. The Bible tells me to be an imitator of God, so I get to imitate Jesus and his glad willingness to submit to the Father's terrible, yet wonderful will. It's the only way I can, through Christ, do everything. Even these awful injections.

Barbara is like the women who followed Christ on his wretched path to Golgotha, mourning and lamenting as they watched their Lord tortured so (Luke 23:27). And although there is no possible way a human can understand the depth of Jesus's anguish—or find language to express it—the lines of this heart-rending hymn, "O Sacred Head, Now Wounded," come close.

Barbara sings them as though she owns them. And she does. She is a wondrous enigma, even to many who know her. Jesus's most ardent followers felt the same about him—he was an enigma; they could not understand how he could make peace with such dreadful suffering. And that's what makes Barbara's eyes shine. For her, it's an affirmation of a fiercely private and passionate resonance with her suffering Savior.

O God, I cling
With feeble fingers to the ledge
Of your great grace, yet feel the wedge
Of this calamity struck hard
Between my chest and this deep-scarred
*And granite precipice of love.**

*John Piper, "Job: Part 2," Desiring God, modified December 4, 1994, https://www.desiringgod.org/.

O SACRED HEAD, NOW WOUNDED

1. O sa - cred Head, now wound - ed, with grief and shame weighed down,
2. What thou, my Lord, hast suf - fered was all for sin - ners' gain.
3. What lan - guage shall I bor - row to thank thee, dear - est Friend,

now scorn - ful - ly sur - round - ed with thorns, thine on - ly crown!
Mine, mine was the trans - gres - sion, but thine the dead - ly pain.
for this, thy dy - ing sor - row, thy pit - y with - out end?

O sa - cred Head, what glo - ry, what bliss till now was thine!
Lo, here I fall, my Sav - ior! 'Tis I de - serve thy place.
Oh, make me thine for - ev - er, and should I faint - ing be,

Yet, though de - spised and gor - y, I joy to call thee mine.
Look on me with thy fa - vor, and grant to me thy grace.
Lord, let me nev - er, nev - er out - live my love to thee.

Words: Medieval Latin, tr. Paul Gerhardt, 1656, and James Alexander, 1830, alt.
Music: Hans Leo Hassler, 1601

HERZLICH TUT
MICH VERLANGEN
76 76 D

16 Faith Is the Victory

Encamped along the hills of light,
Ye Christian soldiers, rise,
And press the battle ere the night
Shall veil the glowing skies.
Against the foe in vales below
Let all our strength be hurled;
Faith is the victory, we know,
That overcomes the world.

Faith is the victory!
Faith is the victory!
O, glorious victory,
That overcomes the world.

His banner over us is love,
Our sword the Word of God;
We tread the road the saints before
With shouts of triumph trod.
By faith, they like a
    whirlwind's breath,
Swept on o'er every field;
The faith by which they
    conquered death
Is still our shining shield. [Refrain]

On every hand the foe we find
Drawn up in dread array;
Let tents of ease be left behind,
And onward to the fray.
Salvation's helmet on each head,
With truth all girt about,
The earth shall tremble
    'neath our tread,
And echo with our shout. [Refrain]

To him that overcomes the foe,
White raiment shall be giv'n;
Before the angels he shall know
His name confessed in heav'n.
Then onward from the hills of light,
Our hearts with love aflame,
We'll vanquish all the hosts of night,
In Jesus' conqu'ring name. [Refrain]

—John Henry Yates (1837–1900)

Faith is the victory . . .
so who's in your foxhole?

No, in all these things we are more than conquerors through him who loved us.
—ROMANS 8:37

"Joni, quick, jump in my foxhole!" It was a text from my friend Shannon Gallatin, and it meant: "My pain is raging; quickly, come to my aid with your prayers!"

When chronic pain mounts an assault against your peace of mind and your resolve to endure, you need a seasoned comrade in arms in your trench. You need a fellow warrior who understands that your laments aren't complaints but appeals for reinforcements against the enemy's wrath. For when his hot-blazing bullets are zinging past your head, there's nothing better than having a battle-savvy veteran to help you repel Satan's advances. I am that reinforcement for Shannon, and she is for me.

Psalm 112 already assures us that we are more than conquerors, for "[those who are righteous] will not be overcome by evil. . . . They do not fear bad news; they confidently trust the LORD to care for them. They are confident and fearless and can face their foes triumphantly" (Ps. 112:6–8 NLT). To be more than a conqueror is to not be overcome by evil, and to not fear bad news, but to confidently trust the Lord!

Like many battered saints in Scripture, Shannon knows how to do this. She has visited the extremes of suffering. She struggles with six chronic diseases, debilitating injuries to her back and neck, and has survived wounds that come from multiple miscarriages. Yet she knows that what God has done *within* her is far more significant than anything done *to* her. She also knows that a decorated soldier cannot do it alone.

The devil is wise to this. It's why you must steward your suffering well, for when you fail at that, when you abandon your station, the enemy steps in to fill the void. He cleverly schemes ways to separate you from those who offer help. He knows that isolation makes you an easy target. Isolation also exacerbates pain—nothing is scarier than feeling alone on the battlefield. So he'll dissuade you from reaching out for help by convincing you that you'd be burdening others, or that no one has it as bad as you.

Satan loathes the esprit de corps between believers in Jesus, so Shannon and I are careful not to drop our shield of faith, not even for a minute. We aim to be the faithful soldiers of which Charles Spurgeon wrote:

> See the Grecian warrior just returned from battle? He has many wounds, and there is a gash across his brow; his breast is streaming here and there with cuts and flesh-wounds; one arm is dislocated. . . . He is covered with the smoke and dust of battle; he is besmeared with [much blood]; he is faint, and weary, and ready to die, but what does he say? As he lifts up his right arm, with his buckler tightly clasped upon it, he cries, "I have fought a good fight, I have kept my shield." That was the object of ambition with every Grecian warrior. If he kept his shield, he came home glorious. Now, faith is the Christian's shield.[30]

There will be times I will fire off a call for reinforcements, and Shannon will radio in with extra prayer. Prayer is, after all, a "wartime walkie-talkie."[31] My trench buddy will also remind me that faith always paves the way to victory. Faith in Christ, the captain of our salvation. Faith in his wartime promises. Faith that Jesus has already defeated the enemy. Faith that V-day is in sight. Faith, in fact, is our victory song:

Then onward from the hills of light,
Our hearts with love aflame,
We'll vanquish all the hosts of night,
In Jesus' conqu'ring name.

Faith is the victory!
Faith is the victory!
O, glorious victory,
That overcomes the world.

Put the trembling hand in His. "We are more than conquerors through Him who loveth us." Come what may, let ills be heaped on ills, He is ours Who can never fail us, the great Captain who never lost a battle yet! Listen, and let the heart be thrilled with new courage as He speaks: "All Power is given unto Me in heaven and in earth: and lo, I am with you alway, even unto the end of the world."*

*Mark Guy Pearse, *The Gentleness of Jesus* (New York: Thomas Y. Crowell, 1898), 186.

FAITH IS THE VICTORY

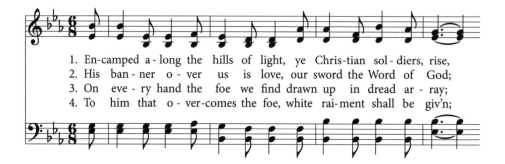

1. En-camped a - long the hills of light, ye Chris-tian sol - diers, rise,
2. His ban - ner o - ver us is love, our sword the Word of God;
3. On eve - ry hand the foe we find drawn up in dread ar - ray;
4. To him that o - ver-comes the foe, white rai - ment shall be giv'n;

and press the bat - tle   ere   the night shall veil   the glow - ing skies.
we   tread the road the saints be - fore with shouts of   tri - umph trod.
let   tents of ease be   left   be - hind, and on - ward to   the fray.
be - fore the an - gels   he shall know his name con - fessed in   heav'n.

A - gainst the foe   in vales be - low   let all our strength be hurled;
By faith, they like   a whirl-wind's breath, swept on   o'er eve - ry field;
Sal - va - tion's hel - met on   each head, with truth all   girt   a - bout,
Then on - ward from the hills   of   light, our hearts with love   a - flame,

faith   is the vic - to - ry,   we know, that o - ver comes the world.
the   faith by which they con - quered death is   still our shin - ing shield.
the   earth shall trem - ble 'neath our tread, and ech - o   with our shout.
we'll van - quish all   the hosts of night, in   Je - sus' con - qu'ring name.

Faith   is the vic - to - ry!   Faith   is the vic - to - ry!

O,   glo - ri - ous vic - to - ry, that o - ver-comes the world.

Words: John H. Yates
Music: Ira D. Sankey

SANKEY
CMD with refrain

PART 3

Songs of Hope

May the God of hope fill you with all joy and
peace in believing, so that by the power of the
Holy Spirit you may abound in hope.

ROMANS 15:13

17   O the Deep, Deep Love of Jesus

O the deep, deep love of Jesus!
Vast, unmeasured, boundless, free,
Rolling as a mighty ocean
In its fullness over me.
Underneath me, all around me,
Is the current of thy love;
Leading onward, leading homeward,
To thy glorious rest above.

O the deep, deep love of Jesus!
Spread his praise from shore to shore;
How he loveth, ever loveth,
Changeth never, nevermore;
How he watcheth o'er his loved ones,
Died to call them all his own;
How for them he intercedeth,
Watcheth o'er them from the throne.

O the deep, deep love of Jesus!
Love of ev'ry love the best:
'Tis an ocean vast of blessing,
'Tis a haven sweet of rest.
O the deep, deep love of Jesus!
'Tis a heav'n of heav'ns to me;
And it lifts me up to glory,
For it lifts me up to thee.

—*Samuel Trevor Francis (1898)*

O the deep, deep love of Jesus . . .
fill my emptiness

Deep calls to deep at the roar of your waterfalls;
all your breakers and your waves have gone over me.
—PSALM 42:7

Fleeing from his enemies, David finds himself somewhere east of the Jordan River, far beyond the walls of Jerusalem. He looks over his shoulder toward the Judean hills, pining for the days when he was able to refresh himself in the courts of the Lord. But there is little time to grieve. The chase is fierce, and trials are coming at him in wave after wave. Stopping to gaze back at "once was," David loses his footing and tumbles under a thrashing waterfall of grief and sadness.

Cut off from the tabernacle, David can only vaguely recall what it was like to worship God with heartfelt joy. Yet even as troubles surge over him in pounding billows, this is a man who refuses to drown.

From a bottomless ocean of sorrow, he cries to God, "Deep calls to deep at the roar of your waterfalls" (Ps. 42:7). Between his emptiness and God's all-sufficiency, David can sense a great gulf. He is desperate to close that gulf, knowing that his profound need can only be answered by a profound remedy. Only the depth of God's almighty fullness can fill his abyss of human need.

It's what "deep calls to deep" means. Notice it is a call, a crying out. A doubling over in anguish, refusing to stifle groans, and loudly pleading, "Why are you cast down, O my soul," and then in the next breath insisting,

"Hope in God!" (42:5). It's when you beg God to pour his deep mercy into your emptiness. And if you must drown, do it under the waterfall of God's almighty fullness!

I cry like that. I groan out loud. When sorrows overwhelm me, I cannot be timid with God. I am too desperate, so I demand that my soul do business, that it confirm its need through deep emotion, that it travail, that it be wholly engaged in its own rescue. I cast myself utterly, completely, and totally on God and his mercy. The deeper my engagement is with him, the greater my assurance of Christ's intimacy in the end. I appeal for God to pour his deep love into my hollowness, often singing through tears:

> O the deep, deep love of Jesus!
> Vast, unmeasured, boundless, free,
> Rolling as a mighty ocean
> In its fullness over me.

This hymn opens the way for a sweeter, more tender intimacy with Jesus. Such closeness does not happen through a solitary trial though; it happens in wave after wave of trials. Faith may be required to *accept* a tribulation, but it takes perseverance to *endure* unending tribulations. Perseverance is faith proved over and over, time and again. Only perseverance can usher you into a beautiful inner sanctum of confidentiality with Jesus, a place where you are never the same.[32]

Thomas Watson once wrote:

> Fervency in prayer is as fire to the incense—it makes it ascend to Heaven as a sweet perfume. To induce believers to pray in faith, let them remember the bountifulness of God. He often exceeds the prayers of His people:
> Hannah asked a son—God gave her not only a son, but a prophet.

Solomon asked wisdom—God gave him not only wisdom, but riches and honor besides. Jacob asked that God would give him food and clothing, but the Lord increased his riches to two bands. The woman of Canaan asked but the life of her child, but Christ not only gave her that—but the life of her soul also![33]

If you find yourself wandering on the other side of "the Jordan" in deep distress, flip open your hymnal to "O the Deep, Deep Love of Jesus." Sing it loudly, as though you were calling out for God to fill you like a mighty ocean. Jesus will then overflow you with deep beauties of his grace and unfathomable mysteries of his loveliness, all the while working in your heart a fresh intimacy that's worth it all.

Did you hear that? He is *worth* it all.

When we shall come home and enter to the possession of our Brother's fair kingdom, and when our heads shall find the weight of the eternal crown of glory, and when we shall look back to pains and sufferings; then shall we see life and sorrow to be less than one step or stride from a prison to glory; and that our little inch of time-suffering is not worthy of our first night's welcome home to heaven.*

*Samuel Rutherford, "The Loveliness of Christ Quotes," GoodReads, accessed July 16, 2021, https://www.goodreads.com/.

O THE DEEP, DEEP LOVE OF JESUS

1. O the deep, deep love of Je-sus! vast, un-meas-ured, bound-less, free,
2. O the deep, deep love of Je-sus! spread his praise from shore to shore;
3. O the deep, deep love of Je-sus! love of ev-'ry love the best:

roll-ing as a might-y o-cean in its full-ness o-ver me.
how he lov-eth, ev-er lov-eth, chang-eth nev-er, nev-er-more;
'tis an o-cean vast of bless-ing, 'tis a ha-ven sweet of rest.

Un-der-neath me, all a-round me, is the cur-rent of thy love;
how he watch-eth o'er his loved ones, died to call them all his own;
O the deep, deep love of Je-sus! 'tis a heav'n of heav'ns to me;

lead-ing on-ward, lead-ing home-ward, to thy glo-rious rest a-bove.
how for them he in-ter-ced-eth, watch-eth o'er them from the throne.
and it lifts me up to glo-ry, for it lifts me up to thee.

Words: S. Trevor Francis, 1898
Music: Thomas J. Williams, 1897

EBENEZER
87 87 D

18 I Must Tell Jesus

I must tell Jesus all of my trials;
I cannot bear these burdens alone;
In my distress he kindly will help me;
He ever loves and cares for his own.

I must tell Jesus!
I must tell Jesus!
I cannot bear my burdens alone;
I must tell Jesus!
I must tell Jesus!
Jesus can help me, Jesus alone.

I must tell Jesus all of my troubles;
He is a kind, compassionate friend;
If I but ask him, he will deliver,
Make of my troubles quickly an end. [Refrain]

Tempted and tried, I need a great Savior,
One who can help my burdens to bear;
I must tell Jesus, I must tell Jesus;
He all my cares and sorrows will share. [Refrain]

O how the world to evil allures me!
O how my heart is tempted to sin!
I must tell Jesus, and he will help me
Over the world the vict'ry to win. [Refrain]

—*Elisha Hoffman (1894)*

I must tell Jesus . . .
how much I need him

Do not be anxious about anything, but in everything by prayer and supplication with thanksgiving let your requests be made known to God.
—PHILIPPIANS 4:6

The last line of "I Must Tell Jesus" simply states, "Jesus can help me, Jesus alone." If Jesus is the only one who can do anything about my needs, he gets an earful from me. I tell him *all* my needs. Every one. But I divide my needs into 20 percent and 80 percent. Twenty percent of the things I tell Jesus about is physical stuff. And 80 percent is for increased faith, fresh courage, an embrace of Jesus and his promises, bright spirits, a singing heart, a larger trust and a bigger hope, the ability to endure, greater patience, concern for others in need, new ways to give the gospel, and thinking on things that are pure, noble, right, just, praiseworthy, and true.

For the life of me, I cannot understand why more people do not pray this way. Often I attend prayer meetings where requests are divvied out for healing, finances, safety in travel, or job promotions. It's natural that people would want prayer for physical things, such as good health, financial blessing, a safe flight, and a better job. But often, those are the only requests I hear. Aren't there deeper and more divinely inspired ways to pray about health, finances, and jobs?

Is there a cancer? Prayer for healing is in order, but so are the robust blessings of Psalm 119:140: "Your promise is well tried, and your servant loves it." How much richer it is to tell Jesus, "Lord, this cancer is testing your promises in the life of my friend who is ill, but you are faithful to every promise you've made to her. May she come to treasure your promises through this time of testing."

Is there a need for finances? Prayer for financial stability may be appropriate, but consider Proverbs 15:17: "Better is a dinner of herbs where love is than a fattened ox and hatred with it." Thus, why not say to Jesus, "Lord, financial blessing isn't the focus; your word says that love should be. May we learn to 'live on little' if it means leaning harder on you as well as each other."

I'm paralyzed. I deal with chronic pain. I still take chemo drugs to battle cancer. I *could* ask people to pray that my oxygen levels stay up while inflammation stays down and that drugs squelch any cancer cells. These are good requests about physical health. But God knows far more about quadriplegia, pain, and cancer than my friends or I ever will, for "your Father knows exactly what you need even before you ask him!" (Matt. 6:8 NLT). The way I see it, God can do miracles with 20 percent of our prayer for physical needs.

It is the 80 percent that's critical. When pain screams for my undivided attention or afflictions hound me, I need endurance, peace of heart, patience, and confidence in God's promises. When I become overwhelmed from lack of sleep, I need perseverance. When my thoughts turn morbid, I need the mental focus to think, *Come on, Joni, God will never leave you nor forsake you, and his strength is made perfect in your weakness.* These virtues are vital; otherwise my physical challenges will defeat me, and we all know "a crushed spirit dries up the bones" (Prov. 17:22).

I must tell Jesus this stuff. And when I sing this hymn, it's my way of telling him how much I need him. Healing and relief from pain? Sure. But 100 percent of my heart just needs—*Jesus.*

The tree of the promise will not drop its fruit, unless shaken by the hand of prayer.*

*Thomas Watson, "Wise and Holy Sayings of Thomas Watson," Grace Gems, accessed July 16, 2021, https://gracegems.org/.

I MUST TELL JESUS

1. I must tell Je - sus all of my tri - als; I can - not
2. I must tell Je - sus all of my trou - bles; he is a
3. Tempt-ed and tried, I need a great Sav - ior, one who can
4. O how the world to e - vil al - lures me! O how my

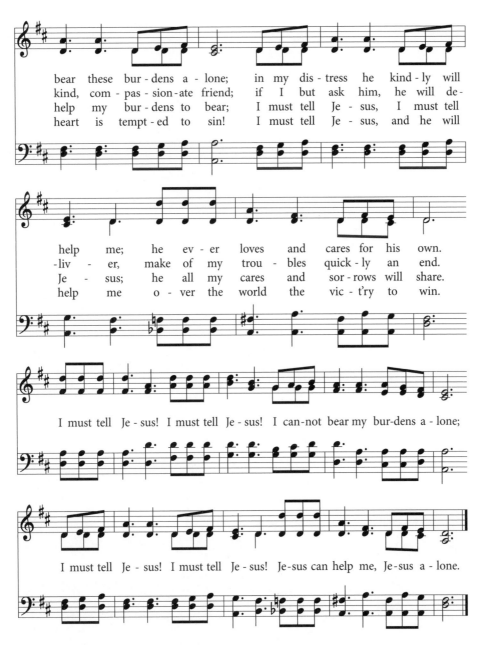

bear these bur-dens a - lone; in my dis-tress he kind-ly will
kind, com - pas - sion-ate friend; if I but ask him, he will de-
help my bur-dens to bear; I must tell Je - sus, I must tell
heart is tempt-ed to sin! I must tell Je - sus, and he will

help me; he ev - er loves and cares for his own.
-liv - er, make of my trou - bles quick - ly an end.
Je - sus; he all my cares and sor-rows will share.
help me o - ver the world the vic - t'ry to win.

I must tell Je - sus! I must tell Je - sus! I can-not bear my bur-dens a - lone;

I must tell Je - sus! I must tell Je - sus! Je-sus can help me, Je-sus a - lone.

Words and Music: Elisha A. Hoffman, 1894

ORWIGSBURG
10 9 10 9 with refrain

19   Come, Thou Long Expected Jesus

Come, thou long-expected Jesus,
Born to set thy people free;
From our fears and sins release us,
Let us find our rest in thee.
Israel's strength and consolation,
Hope of all the earth thou art;
Dear desire of every nation,
Joy of every longing heart.

Born thy people to deliver,
Born a child and yet a king,
Born to reign in us for ever,
Now thy gracious kingdom bring.
By thine own eternal Spirit
Rule in all our hearts alone;
By thine all-sufficient merit,
Raise us to thy glorious throne.

—*Charles Wesley (1745)*

Come, thou long expected Jesus . . .
I am waiting on you

And all these, though commended through their faith,
did not receive what was promised.
—HEBREWS 11:39

How long does it take for a dream to come true? When do you stop believing that a promise will be fulfilled? Think about it. How long will you wait for a promise to be met before you stop believing? Months? Years?

Try hundreds of years. If you leaf through the pages of the Old Testament and into the New, you will find that people hung on to the promise of God for a long, long time. God announced his intentions about the Messiah when he made a promise to Abraham. And what did Abraham do? He believed that God would come through on his promise—and Abraham's confidence in God was credited to him as righteousness.

But I wonder how Abraham felt many years later. How did his children and grandchildren feel many more years later? Where was this promised Messiah? How long did people wait before they finally stopped believing? The fact is, many did stop. "God's not a promise keeper," they huffed.

But others continued to believe. They dreamed of the day when God's promise would be fulfilled. These were the ones who recognized Christ's coming when it happened. Take Zechariah in the Gospel of Luke. Right before the promised Messiah was born, Zechariah happily sang, "Praise be to the Lord, the God of Israel, because he has come. . . . As he said [he would] through his holy prophets of long ago . . . to remember his holy [promise] . . . [that] he swore to our father Abraham" (Luke 1:68–73 NIV).

Zechariah, and many like him, did not stop believing. Maybe that's why you and I feel such *nostalgic* longings when Advent season rolls around. What are our hearts longing for? We are aching to experience God's promises in their totality. For although Christ our Savior came into the world—although we have citizenship in heaven and the promise of grace upon grace to meet our needs—*still* we live in a world of sin. Yes, Jesus has freed us from its power, but not from its presence.

We still wrestle with pain and become easily discouraged. We have questions about suffering that seem unanswerable, and we struggle to stay satisfied in God. Even when we read the many promises of God, they often feel out of reach. When that happens, we are separating God's promises from the promised one, "For all the promises of God find their Yes in [Jesus]" (2 Cor. 1:20).

If we long for peace in our sorrow, Jesus is the Prince of Peace. If we are aching for hope beyond our afflictions, he is the God of all hope. If we yearn for patience and endurance when they seem out of reach, he is the God of endurance. Jesus is the God of all comfort. Every grace and hardship find their source in the Lord of grace (Isa. 9:6; Rom. 15:5, 13; 2 Cor. 1:3; 1 Pet. 5:10).

You may be suffering, but do not stop singing. Do not stop believing. The long-expected one has come (and has promised that he is on his way back)! You can bank on every single one of his promises because Christ sealed them with his blood. So turn to him in your pain, for the promise maker *always* makes good on his word.

*Affliction is a pill, which, being wrapt up in patience and quiet
submission, may be easily swallowed; but discontent chews the pill,
and so embitters the soul.**

*John Flavel, "John Flavel Quotes," AZ Quotes, accessed July 16, 2021, https://www.azquotes.com/.

COME, THOU LONG EXPECTED JESUS

1. Come, thou long-ex-pect-ed Je-sus, born to set thy
2. Born thy peo-ple to de-liv-er, born a child and

peo-ple free; from our fears and sins re-lease us,
yet a king, born to reign in us for ev-er,

let us find our rest in thee. Is-rael's strength and con-so-
now thy gra-cious king-dom bring. By thine own e-ter-nal

-la-tion, hope of all the earth thou art; dear de-sire of
Spir-it rule in all our hearts a-lone; by thine all-suf-

eve-ry na-tion, joy of eve-ry long-ing heart.
-fi-cient mer-it, raise us to thy glo-rious throne.

Words: Charles Wesley, 1745
Music: Rowland Prichard, 1844

HYFRYDOL
87 87 D

20   Standing on the Promises

Standing on the promises of Christ my King,
Through eternal ages let his praises ring;
Glory in the highest, I will shout and sing,
Standing on the promises of God.

Standing, standing,
Standing on the promises of God my Savior;
Standing, standing,
I'm standing on the promises of God.

Standing on the promises that cannot fail,
When the howling storms of doubt and fear assail,
By the living Word of God I shall prevail,
Standing on the promises of God. [Refrain]

Standing on the promises I now can see
Perfect, present cleansing in the blood for me;
Standing in the liberty where Christ makes free,
Standing on the promises of God. [Refrain]

Standing on the promises of Christ the Lord,
Bound to him eternally by love's strong cord,
Overcoming daily with the Spirit's sword,
Standing on the promises of God. [Refrain]

—*Russell Kelso Carter (1886)*

Standing on the promises . . .
they never fail me

This is my comfort in my affliction, that your promise gives me life.
—PSALM 119:50

Afflictions change everything. Even the way we sing this hymn. I used to belt out "Standing on the Promises" like a happy Baptist at Saturday night revival. Now, I sing it from my wheelchair more slowly, thinking through the words—and the promises.

The other morning, I woke up with a deep cramp in my hip. I got dressed and wheeled into the van to go to work, but halfway down the freeway, I almost asked my husband to turn around and take me home. I was in unbearable pain. *I think you are asking too much of me*, I said to God in my head. *You are asking the impossible—I don't think I can do this.*

In his rearview mirror, Ken could see my look of desperation. Not wanting to trouble him or abort our plans for the day, I avoided the mirror, lowered my head, and whimpered, "But God, you obviously think I can do this. So where is the help you promise?" The word *promise* triggered Psalm 119:50: "This is my comfort in my affliction, that your promise gives me life." *Joni, there's your help*, the Spirit seemed to whisper. God's promises. Stand on the promises of Christ your King.

That did it. I began repeating out loud every Scripture promise I could recall, voicing them above the freeway noise so that Ken could hear me: "Lord, you promise that you are my ever-present help in this trouble. You promise that your grace is more than sufficient for this need. You promise not to leave or forsake me." It was a tumble of words that drew an odd look from Ken, but also a smile. He knew what I was doing.

"If I stand firm to the end, you promise you'll save me; you give strength to the weary; I shall see the goodness of the Lord in the land of the living." I was now shouting, "God, I'm running to you; your name is a strong tower. Jesus, you say that everything is possible with your grace, so please help me do the impossible. Help me get *through* this." I kept repeating Bible promises for the next five miles.

When we arrived at the office, something was different. My anguish had not lessened, but I had courage. Now, some people might say my rapid-fire litany only served to distract me from my misery. But I knew better. God came through on his promises. He renewed me. Refreshed me. Encouraged me. His promises helped me do the impossible, and I no longer felt defeated.

I got out of the van, wheeled through the office door, and sang as I went up the ramp. Everyone on the first floor could hear me belting out "Standing on the Promises" like a happy Baptist at Saturday night revival. To me, Charles Spurgeon nails what happened that day:

> The precious promises of our great God are distinctly intended to be taken to him and exchanged for the blessings which they guarantee. . . . Take care how you pray. Make real business of it. . . . [Some] do not plead the promise in a truthful . . . way. What is prayer but the promise pleaded? A promise is, so to speak, the raw material of prayer. Prayer irrigates the fields of life with the waters which are stored up in the reservoirs of promise. The promise is the power of prayer. We go to God, and we say to him, "Do as you have said. O Lord, here is your Word; we ask you to fulfill it."[34]

That day in the van, God did.

That prayer is most likely to pierce Heaven, which first pierces one's own heart. Prayer without fervency is no prayer. Lifeless prayer is no more prayer than the picture of a man, is a man.*

*Watson, "Thomas Watson's Choice Quotes on Prayer," Grace Gems, accessed July 16, 2021.

STANDING ON THE PROMISES

1. Stand-ing on the prom-is-es of Christ my King, thro' e-ter-nal a-ges
2. Stand-ing on the prom-is-es that can-not fail, when the howl-ing storms of
3. Stand-ing on the prom-is-es I now can see per-fect, pres-ent clean-sing
4. Stand-ing on the prom-is-es of Christ the Lord, bound to him e-ter-nal-

let his prais-es ring; glo-ry in the high-est, I will shout and sing,
doubt and fear as-sail, by the liv-ing Word of God I shall pre-vail,
in the blood for me; stand-ing in the lib-er-ty where Christ makes free,
-ly by love's strong cord, o-ver-com-ing dai-ly with the Spir-it's sword,

stand-ing on the prom-is-es of God. Stand-ing, stand-ing,

stand-ing on the prom-is-es of God my Sav-ior; stand-ing,

stand-ing, I'm stand-ing on the prom-is-es of God.

Words and Music: Russell Kelso Carter, 1886

21 Guide Me, O Thou Great Jehovah

Guide me, O thou great Jehovah,
Pilgrim through this barren land;
I am weak, but thou art mighty;
Hold me with thy pow'rful hand.
Bread of heaven, Bread of heaven,
Feed me till I want no more;
Feed me till I want no more.

Open now the crystal fountain,
Whence the healing stream doth flow.
Let the fire and cloudy pillar
Lead me all my journey through.
Strong Deliv'rer, strong Deliv'rer,
Be thou still my strength and shield,
Be thou still my strength and shield.

Lord, I trust thy mighty power,
Wondrous are thy works of old;
Thou deliver'st thine from thralldom,
Who for naught themselves had sold:
Thou didst conquer, thou
    didst conquer
Sin and Satan and the grave,
Sin and Satan and the grave.

When I tread the verge of Jordan,
Bid my anxious fears subside.
Death of death, and hell's
    Destruction,
Land me safe on Canaan's side.
Songs of praises, songs of praises
I will ever give to thee;
I will ever give to thee.

—*William Williams (1762/1771)*

Guide me, O thou great Jehovah . . .
my pilgrim journey is hard

But you have come to Mount Zion and to the city of the living God,
the heavenly Jerusalem, and to innumerable angels in festal gathering.
—HEBREWS 12:22

God's people have always sung pilgrim songs. On a long road trip, everyone likes a good song that passes the time. Joseph, Mary, and Jesus would have done the same as they traveled in caravans with neighbors and relatives to attend yearly festivals—the boy Jesus probably learned all of the pilgrim songs by heart. He recited these same ancient songs with his disciples as they walked the dirt paths and dry streambeds from Galilee to celebrate the Jewish Passover. These festival songs were known as the Psalms of Ascent, the title given to Psalms 120 through 134. Every good pilgrim knew them.

To what were the pilgrims ascending, and why sing about it? They were literally and figuratively ascending, or going up, to worship in the city of the great King. Jerusalem is built on top of a mountain ridge, the highest point of which is the temple, on the summit, so we can picture weary pilgrims, traveling from as far away as the edge of Turkey, always scanning the horizon to spot the tips of citadels on Mount Zion.

Psalms of Ascent contain great truths that informed a traveler's pilgrimage. Although they are hopeful, a pilgrim started his journey with Psalm 120, a song that begins with a call of distress, a confession that he is a sojourner in a troubled, broken land: "Too long have I had my dwelling among those who hate peace" (Ps. 120:6).[35]

It is possible that Jesus sang this verse, Psalm 120:6, on his final pilgrimage to Jerusalem. I can picture him and his disciples setting out from Jericho in the morning for the long, tiring trek up the winding dirt road to the holy city. The others did not realize this would be Jesus's final Passover. Yet even with the specter of a Roman cross filling his vision, it is no stretch to think that he still sang the songs of Zion as he walked, beginning with Psalm 120. As he anticipated the cries for his crucifixion, he may have even felt the weight of dwelling "too long among those who hate peace."

"Guide Me, O Thou Great Jehovah" is, for me, a modern-day song of ascent. We are all pilgrims on a hard road through a troubled land where suffering can make the journey feel interminably long. Still, we are heading *up*. We are looking up. We are traveling up to "the city of the living God, the heavenly Jerusalem. You have come . . . in joyful assembly" (Heb. 12:22 NIV). We are scanning the horizon to spot the tips of citadels on Mount Zion, and so we sing:

> Guide me, O thou great Jehovah,
> Pilgrim through this barren land;
> I am weak, but thou art mighty;
> Hold me with thy pow'rful hand.
> Bread of heaven, Bread of heaven,
> Feed me till I want no more;
> Feed me till I want no more.

It takes supernatural effort to keep putting one weary foot in front of the other, all the while fixing your focus on your heavenly destination. Perhaps you are asking the question in Psalm 137:4, "How shall we sing the LORD's song in a foreign land?" If so, then be encouraged by these words from Percy Ainsworth: "The only place where a man can learn to sing the Lord's song as it should be sung [is] in the strange land. . . . There is a sense in which the learning and the singing are one."[36]

Train your heart to sing the Lord's songs in a troubled, broken land. It's how songs of faith should be sung—always with your face toward the holy city.

---

*The countries far north are cold and frozen because they are distant from the sun. What makes such frozen, uncomfortable Christians, but their living so far from heaven? And what makes others so warm, but their living higher, and having nearer access to God?**

*Richard Baxter, "The Suburbs of Heaven," The Reformed Reader, accessed July 16, 2021, http://www.reformedreader.org/.

GUIDE ME, O THOU GREAT JEHOVAH

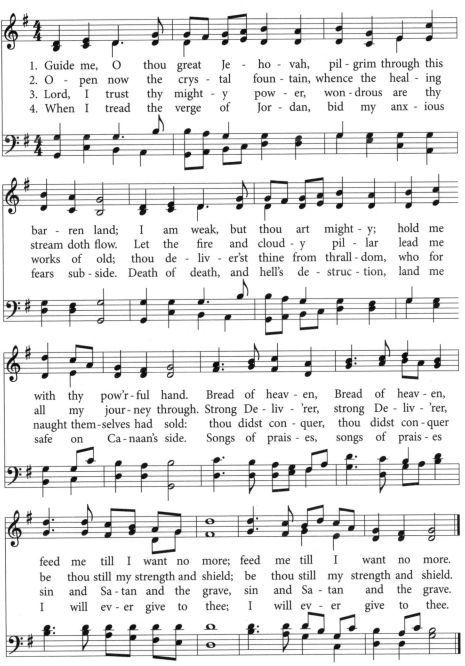

Words: William Williams, 1762/1771; st. 1 tr. Peter Williams, 1771, alt.
Music: John Hughes, 1907

CWM RHONDDA
87 87 87 7

22   For All the Saints

For all the saints, who from
    their labors rest,
Who thee by faith before
    the world confessed,
Thy name, O Jesus, be forever bless'd.
Alleluia, alleluia!

Thou wast their rock, their
    refuge, and their might,
Thou, Christ, the hope that
    put their fears to flight;
'Mid gloom and doubt, their
    true and shining light.
Alleluia, alleluia!

Oh, bless'd communion,
    fellowship divine!
We feebly struggle, they
    in glory shine,
Yet all are one in thee,
    for all are thine.
Alleluia, alleluia!

The golden evening brightens
    in the west.
Soon, soon to faithful
    servants cometh rest.
Sweet is the calm of
    paradise the bless'd.
Alleluia, alleluia!

But lo! There breaks a yet
    more glorious day;
the saints triumphant rise
    in bright array,
as God to glory calls them all away.
Alleluia, alleluia!

From earth's wide bounds, from
    ocean's farthest coast,
Through gates of pearl streams
    in the countless host,
All praising Father, Son,
    and Holy Ghost.
Alleluia, alleluia!

—*William Walsham How (1864)*

For all the saints . . .
on whose shoulders we stand

Be imitators of me, as I am of Christ.
—1 CORINTHIANS 11:1

I wheeled onto the stage at Wheaton College, scarcely believing I had the privilege of giving the address at Elisabeth Elliot's memorial service. Ever since high school, I'd been captivated by the story of the twenty-nine-year-old jungle missionary whose husband of less than three years had been savagely speared to death by the Stone Age people he tried to reach for Christ. What drove her to go back to that tribe with her baby, a Bible, and a snakebite kit to bring the gospel to the very men who had murdered her beloved? Was Jesus worth it?

After high school, I asked myself the same question when a broken neck led me into those dark valleys that Elisabeth had written about. Sitting in my wheelchair, I worked my way through her books. I, too, had to know if Jesus is worth it. I found that she didn't skate the surface—she convinced me that her Savior is ecstasy beyond compare. After reading almost all her works, I heard Jesus whisper in my heart, "Be like her."

I strived to imitate Elisabeth, as she imitated Christ. She believed that the Bible's answers should not be separated from the God of the Bible; she believed that a mechanistic approach to suffering holds no relief. If anything, all the numerous "reasons" why God allows suffering held only disappointment. On the other hand, being shoved messily against Jesus's breast was a reservoir of hope and help. So I came to terms with suffering the way she did—through an earnest grappling with the angel of the Lord in which he finally prevailed.

Many young people do not recognize the name Elisabeth Elliot. Nowadays, everyone's story is extraordinary, whether it has the stamp of Christ or not. Courage is rare. Good character, rarer. Even Christians feel that suffering should be mitigated at all costs. And if it cannot be avoided, it must be drugged, divorced, escaped from, or prayed away. Yet I think people still crave husky, authentic examples of faith. Thomas Brooks wrote:

> Set the highest examples and patterns before your face of grace and godliness for your imitation. In the business of faith, set an Abraham before your eyes. In the business of courage, set a Joshua. In the business of uprightness, set a Job. Of meekness, a Moses, and so on. There is a disadvantage . . . in looking more backwards than forwards. Men look on whom they excel, not on those of whom they fall short. Next to Christ, set the pattern of the choicest saints before you.[37]

"For All the Saints" speaks of those very people. So when eighty-eight-year-old Elisabeth died, most of her admirers were relieved that she was finally free from her dementia, while others wept over the loss of a great saint. When I heard the news of her passing, I put down everything, stopped, and sang this classical hymn. I sang it again at Wheaton College as the concluding touch to my message, inviting the audience to join me in honor of our departed friend.

> Oh, bless'd communion, fellowship divine!
> We feebly struggle, they in glory shine.

You are not the first on God's forge of affliction. Others like Elisabeth Elliot have gone before, leaving you many convincing examples to imitate.

If Elisabeth's story moves you, and you hear the Spirit whispering, "Be like her," you can begin right now by memorizing the words to this, one of her favorite hymns.

We comfort others truly, when we make them stronger to endure, when we put courage into their hearts, when we enable them to pass through their sorrow victoriously. That is the way Christ comforts. He does not merely sit down beside troubled ones and enter into their experiences. He does sympathize with them—but it is that he may make them strong to endure.*

*J. R. Miller, "Things to Live For: Chapter 17—The Beatitude of Sorrow," O Christian, accessed July 16, 2021, http://articles.ochristian.com/.

FOR ALL THE SAINTS

1. For all the saints, who from their la-bors rest, who thee by
2. Thou wast their rock, their ref-uge, and their might, thou, Christ, the
3. Oh, bless'd com-mun-ion, fel-low-ship di-vine! We feeb-ly
4. The gold-en eve-ning bright-ens in the west. Soon, soon to

faith be-fore the world con-fessed, thy name, O Je-sus, be for-
hope that put their fears to flight; 'mid gloom and doubt, their true and
strug-gle, they in glo-ry shine, yet all are one in thee, for
faith-ful ser-vants com-eth rest. Sweet is the calm of par-a-

al - le-lu - ia!

-ev - er bless'd.
shin-ing light. Al - le-lu - ia, al - le-lu - ia!
all are thine.
-dise the bless'd.

5. But lo! There breaks
   a yet more glorious day;
   the saints triumphant rise in bright array,
   as God to glory calls them all away.
   Alleluia, alleluia!

6. From earth's wide bounds,
   from ocean's farthest coast,
   through gates of pearl
   streams in the countless host,
   all praising Father, Son, and Holy Ghost.
   Alleluia, alleluia!

Words: William How, 1864, alt.
Music: Ralph Vaughan Williams, 1906

SINE NOMINE
10 10 10 with alleluias

23   Far from My Heavenly Home

Far from my heav'nly home,
Far from my Father's breast,
Fainting I cry, blest Spirit, come,
And speed me to my rest.

My spirit homeward turns,
And fain would thither flee:
My heart, O Zion, droops and yearns,
When I remember thee.

To thee, to thee I press,
A dark and toilsome road:
When shall I pass the wilderness,
And reach the saints' abode?

God of my life, be near;
On thee my hopes I cast:
O guide me through the desert here,
And bring me home at last.

—Henry Francis Lyte (1834)

Far from my heavenly home . . .
next stop: heaven

These all died in faith, not having received the things promised, but having seen them and greeted them from afar, and having acknowledged that they were strangers and exiles on the earth. For people who speak thus make it clear that they are seeking a homeland.
—HEBREWS 11:13–14

Like the people of faith mentioned in Hebrews 11, I am happy to call myself an exile, a stranger, a nomad here on earth. Obviously, people who say such things don't feel quite at home here; they are looking forward to a country they can call their own. A homeland for their soul.

Whenever I run across a Christian who thinks this way, I know I've found a kindred spirit. Like twenty-year-old Michele. I met her when we were at a funeral for her father, who had passed from cancer. As I was wheeling away from the graveside service, Michele ran up to thank me for coming. She then shared a remarkable conversation she'd had with her dad the day before he died.

"My father was restless and unable to let go," she said. "I was sitting by his bedside, and I told him, 'Daddy, it's okay. You can let go.' He gathered his strength and said, 'But, honey, I won't be here to walk you down the aisle.'"

Michele wasn't even engaged to be married. It hurt to watch her father needlessly pile anxiety on top of his physical pain, so Michele tenderly held his hand and whispered, "Oh, Daddy, please don't worry about my wedding. Don't let that distress you. After all, you're a man of Hebrews 11. You're heading for a better country, a homeland in heaven. There's nothing to miss about my earthly wedding. My dress will fade and become torn. My wedding photos will yellow with age. My body will grow old and turn to dust. But everything in heaven will last forever, and I will meet you at the real wedding on the other side!"

Her father immediately relaxed. A knowing smile crossed his face, and he weakly nodded. What she said was true. He was heading for a *far* better country. The next day Michele's father peacefully stepped into the other side of eternity.

Somehow this daughter found the composure to say not only fitting words to her father, but true and *selfless* ones. She didn't dwell on things *she* would miss, like her dad not being around to walk her down the aisle; rather, Michele focused on what her father's soul needed to hear at that moment. True words. Powerful Hebrews 11 words. Because her wedding dress *will* fade, and her body *will* turn to dust. These are facts we need to rehearse every day.

When affliction forces my eyes upward and I strain to see what is unseen, when I need to interpret my pain in light of eternity, this is the hymn I turn to: "God of my life, be near; on thee my hopes I cast: O guide me through the desert here, and bring me home at last."

Compared to eternity, our grief is only a moment in time. The saddest heart can be assured that "this light momentary affliction is preparing for us an eternal weight of glory beyond all comparison, as we look not to the things that are seen but to the things that are unseen. For the things that are seen are transient, but the things that are unseen are eternal" (2 Cor. 4:17–18).

So while you work to bring Christ's kingdom to earth, remember that its capital city is in another land. Keep your eyes scanning for heaven's horizon. You'll be home soon.

Let us press forward to that which is before, leaving earth and earthly matters more and more, and yielding ourselves more fully to the cords which draw us towards the celestial country. Let us cry, "Heavenward, ho!" Pull up the anchor, spread the sails, and let us go away to the fair country wither Jesus has gone before us.*

*Charles Spurgeon, "Forty Years," Christian Classics Ethereal Library, accessed June 2, 2021, https://ccel.org/.

FAR FROM MY HEAVENLY HOME

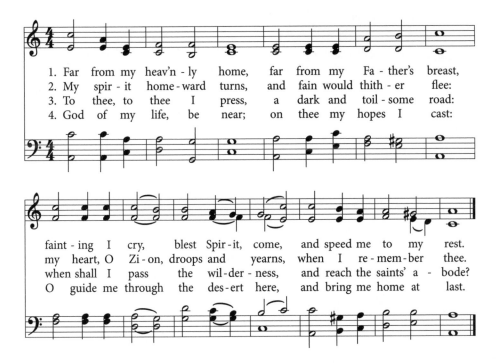

1. Far from my heav'n-ly home, far from my Fa-ther's breast,
2. My spir-it home-ward turns, and fain would thith-er flee:
3. To thee, to thee I press, a dark and toil-some road:
4. God of my life, be near; on thee my hopes I cast:

faint-ing I cry, blest Spir-it, come, and speed me to my rest.
my heart, O Zi-on, droops and yearns, when I re-mem-ber thee.
when shall I pass the wil-der-ness, and reach the saints' a-bode?
O guide me through the des-ert here, and bring me home at last.

Words: Henry Francis Lyte, 1834
Music: John Bernard Wilkes, 1861

LYTE
SM

24 Face to Face with Christ, My Savior

Face to face with Christ, my Savior,
Face to face—what will it be
When with rapture I behold him,
Jesus Christ who died for me?

Face to face I shall behold him,
Far beyond the starry sky;
Face to face in all his glory,
I shall see him by and by!

Only faintly now I see him
With the darkened veil between,
But a blessed day is coming
When his glory shall be seen. [Refrain]

What rejoicing in his presence,
When are banished grief and pain;
When the crooked ways are straightened
And the dark things shall be plain. [Refrain]

Face to face—oh, blissful moment!
Face to face—to see and know;
Face to face with my Redeemer
Jesus Christ who loves me so. [Refrain]

—*Carrie Ellis Breck (1898)*

Face to face with Christ, my Savior . . .
the lover of my soul

Such is the generation of those who seek him,
who seek the face of the God of Jacob.
—PSALM 24:6

I long to see the face of my Savior.

Deep down inside, you do too. We find it hard to rest comfortably in a relationship—with God, or anyone—when we cannot see their face. The essence of a person is in his face, eyes, mouth, and smile. It is why most of us were so frustrated with COVID requirements about wearing masks. Everyone's faces were hidden.

Lovers understand the magnetic pull of their beloved's face. When separated, they are always gazing at photos of each other. Their loved one's face represents everything they adore, and they count the days until they can be together again.

Like a tenderhearted lover, God pulls us in the same magnetic way, saying, "Seek my face," and we rise to respond, "Your face, LORD, do I seek" (Ps. 27:8). Our suffering awakens even greater tenderness in Christ, for "the LORD is near to the brokenhearted and saves the crushed in spirit" (Ps. 34:18). A sufferer cannot help but sense this and responds under the Lord's sweet smile, drawn into his eyes of compassion (Num. 6:25; Ps. 33:18). A sufferer is sensitive to the Lord's loving touch, for "though I walk in the midst of trouble . . . your right hand delivers me" (Ps. 138:7). Suffering has the capacity to mysteriously strengthen the love we have for our Lord!

Pain pal Barbara Coleman experiences such intimacy with Jesus, even though she struggles with degenerative disc disease, lymphoma, Lyme disease, fibromyalgia, and more. She writes, "My world is smaller, but the Lord is larger. When I wake up, before looking at my own face in the mirror, I look to the Lord and ask him to wash all my sins away so I can start fresh. Throughout the day I remember his tender love, and at night when I lie down, I can feel 'his left arm under my head and his right arm embraces me' (Song 2:6). Sometimes in bed, I will cry from incomprehensible happiness; it's a joy that grips me harder than my pain. I'm just so *happy* to be near the King!"

It's the kind of intimacy described in Song of Solomon 8:5: "Who is that coming up from the wilderness, leaning on her beloved?" Spurgeon explains:

> There can be no leaning on another unless we believe in that other's presence and nearness.... We lean because we are weak.... Because the way is long. Life is a wilderness and we lean because the road is perilous. We lean on our Beloved because the route is ascending, "Coming up." The Christian's way is up . . . the tendency of man's nature is downward. . . . Christ is higher than we are; if we lean, we shall rise.[38]

Although I suffer with far fewer things than Barbara, I am, like her, often swept away with happiness when I'm in bed with pain. Sometimes I cannot tell if my tears flow from agony or from my joy in the Lord. Whichever, in the evening light of my bedroom I lean on my beloved, ascending on my perilous way, climbing higher and singing:

> Face to face I shall behold him,
> Far beyond the starry sky;
> Face to face in all his glory,
> I shall see him by and by.

This hymn describes the breathless moment when "we shall be like him, because we shall see him as he is" (1 John 3:2). So when suffering makes your world small, remember that the Lord is larger. Discover how much larger by pondering the words to this hymn. Sing it as you "look to the LORD and his strength; seek his face always" (Ps. 105:4 NIV), and then dream of the day you will be melded with Christ into the deepest union possible.

It's what every lover longs for.

The winter prepares the earth for the spring—so do afflictions sanctified prepare the soul for glory.*

*Richard Sibbes, "Pithy Puritan Quotes," Grace Gems, accessed July 16, 2021, https://www.gracegems.org/.

FACE TO FACE WITH CHRIST, MY SAVIOR

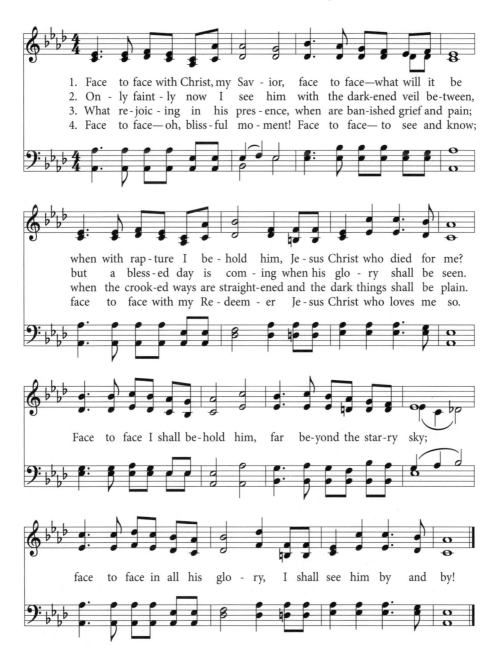

1. Face to face with Christ, my Sav-ior, face to face—what will it be
2. On-ly faint-ly now I see him with the dark-ened veil be-tween,
3. What re-joic-ing in his pres-ence, when are ban-ished grief and pain;
4. Face to face—oh, bliss-ful mo-ment! Face to face— to see and know;

when with rap-ture I be-hold him, Je-sus Christ who died for me?
but a bless-ed day is com-ing when his glo-ry shall be seen.
when the crook-ed ways are straight-ened and the dark things shall be plain.
face to face with my Re-deem-er Je-sus Christ who loves me so.

Face to face I shall be-hold him, far be-yond the star-ry sky;

face to face in all his glo-ry, I shall see him by and by!

Words: Carrie E. Breck, 1898
Music: Grant Colfax Tullar, 1898

FACE TO FACE
87 87 D

25   When We All Get to Heaven

Sing the wondrous love of Jesus,
Sing his mercy and his grace;
In the mansions bright and blessed
He'll prepare for us a place.

When we all get to heaven,
what a day of rejoicing that will be!
When we all see Jesus,
we'll sing and shout the victory!

While we walk the pilgrim pathway
Clouds will overspread the sky;
But when trav'ling days are over
Not a shadow, not a sigh. [Refrain]

Let us then be true and faithful,
Trusting, serving ev'ry day;
Just one glimpse of him in glory
Will the toils of life repay. [Refrain]

Onward to the prize before us!
Soon his beauty we'll behold;
Soon the pearly gates will open—
We shall tread the streets of gold. [Refrain]

—*Eliza Edmunds Hewitt (1898)*

When we all get to heaven . . .
what a day of rejoicing that will be!

The Spirit and the Bride say, "Come."
—REVELATION 22:17

With every decade of quadriplegia that passes, my longing for heaven grows fonder. Some people think I want Jesus to return soon so I can jump out of my wheelchair and walk again. But leaning on my Savior has driven my longings deeper. A glorified body will be nice, but I want a pure heart.

I am so sick and tired of sin. I am weary of constantly battling dark temptations that try to convince me that "my load is too heavy." I am weary of scowling when a heavy marine layer makes my joints scream. I am tired of hearing the devil say, "You deserve a little bitterness today; just look at all you go through!" Sin infects everything. It is even at the root of strange, new illnesses that ravage others' bodies and spirits. My heart aches when I hear of people giving up because of unbearable suffering. Some choosing even suicide.

Oh, come soon, Lord Jesus!

Surely in your own afflictions, you feel the same. But, oh, what if we are blessed to be living at the time of Christ's return? We will literally hear "the Lord . . . descend from heaven with a cry of command," and the bridegroom will rescue, redeem, and restore (1 Thess. 4:16).

We are now getting to the heart of why we long for Jesus's return: it will be the end of the ages, a closing of the curtain on sin, suffering, and Satan. Christ's kingdom will be complete. His matchless name vindicated. Death and the devil and his hordes—all of them—judged and destroyed. The glory of Jesus Christ filling the universe as he is crowned King of kings. Earth and heaven, free of sin and decay.

At this, our faces may grow hot and our hearts may pound, for in a flash we shall be glorified. Shining in brilliant beauty, with no more pain or sorrow, dementia, or disability. We will shed these travails as we would a heavy coat slipping from our shoulders, and we'll finally comprehend that the whole plan of redemption—all the suffering—was the Father's way of securing for his Son a wonderful gift: a radiant bride. And to think we can brighten that radiance, for it will be made plain how our suffering prepared us for such shining glory! Charles Spurgeon writes:

> We make too much of this poor life, for the trials that now weigh us down will soon vanish like morning dew. We are only here long enough to feel an April shower of pain, then we are gone among the unfading flowers of the endless May. So, put things in order. Allot to this brief life its brief consideration, and to everlasting glory, its weight of happy meditations.[39]

Now picture it. You and I among great multitudes of the redeemed, pulsing with joy and infused with light. We are surrounded by the angelic host, and we happily press in line with the great procession of the saved, streaming through gates of pearl, an infinite cavalcade from earth's wide bounds and the oceans' farthest coasts, all in one joyous parade—countless generations, all lifting our diadems before God.

I was able to glimpse through a glass darkly this very moment when, at the Getty SING! 2019 Conference, I led the audience in singing "When We All Get to Heaven." The rousing a cappella, four-part harmony of more than four thousand believers literally shook the floor beneath my wheelchair. Although I was supposed to be leading, I stopped at the third stanza and simply bathed in the moment. I was overwhelmed by the thought, "Just one glimpse of him in glory will the toils of life repay."

When we all get to heaven, what a day of rejoicing that will be. Saint Sebastian said, "When it is all over you will not regret having suffered; rather you will regret having suffered so little, and suffered that little, so badly." So lift your triumphant songs of affliction to the Lord, and make yourself ready. Sing, "Come, Lord Jesus and carry your Bride across your threshold, making all things even us—new."[40]

---

*Consider that the trials and troubles, the calamities and miseries, the crosses and losses that you meet with in this world, are all the hell that ever you shall have.**

*Thomas Brooks, "Words of Wisdom by Thomas Brooks," Hail & Fire Books, accessed July 16, 2021, https://www.hailandfire.com/.

WHEN WE ALL GET TO HEAVEN

1. Sing the won-drous love of Je - sus, sing his mer - cy
2. While we walk the pil - grim path - way, clouds will o - ver -
3. Let us then be true and faith - ful, trust - ing, serv - ing
4. On - ward to the prize be - fore us! Soon his beau - ty

and his grace; in the man - sions bright and bless - ed,
-spread the sky; but when trav - 'ling days are o - ver,
ev - 'ry day; just one glimpse of him in glo - ry
we'll be - hold; soon the pearl - y gates will o - pen—

he'll pre - pare for us a place.
not a shad-ow, not a sigh.   When we all   get to
will the toils of life re - pay.
we shall tread the streets of gold.   When we all
1. for   us a place.   When we all

heav - en, what a day of re - joic-ing that will be!   When we
what a day   of re - joic-ing that will be!

all   see Je - sus, we'll sing and shout the vic - to - ry.
when we all   and   shout the vic - to - ry.

Words: Eliza E. Hewitt, 1898; Music: Emily D. Wilson, 1898

HEAVEN
87 87 with refrain

A Reprise

A reprise is a musical reflection, usually at the end of a song. So allow me to share a reflection or two before you close this book.

No thinking person invites suffering into his or her life. God would not want us to even pray for such a thing. He's written enough troubles into the script of our lives without us asking for them. Yet when trouble does arrive, it can evoke the most poignant and powerful music. Saint Augustine knew this. Although he lived between AD 354 and 430, he wrote with modern clarity:

> God of our life, there are days when the burdens we carry chafe our shoulders and weigh us down; when the road seems dreary and endless, the skies gray and threatening; when our lives have no music in them, and our hearts are lonely and our souls have lost courage. Flood the path with light, we beseech Thee; turn our eyes to where the skies are full of promise; tune our hearts to brave music; give us the sense of comradeship with heroes and saints of every age; and so quicken our spirits that we may be able to encourage the souls of all who journey with us on the road of life, to Thy honor and glory.[41]

I hope you have found brave music in this little book, courageous music that tunes your heart to sing God's praises through suffering. And should you desire to carry the song with you, I encourage you to do the following:

- Memorize as many of these timeless hymns as possible. On my ministry trips, I always print out the words of a new hymn and learn it while "on the road"—on an airplane, waiting in a hotel lobby, or driving in a van.

- Learn the tune by hunting down the hymn online. Don't forget that our minds are programmed to remember patterns in music better than we remember patterns in words alone.

- Print out the words and make each song a prayer. Day or night, weave the rich vocabulary of these stanzas into your praise to God, your petitions, and your intercessions for his people.

- Create a folder so you can keep adding to your collection of hymns memorized. Then the next time your life script encounters a new trouble, you'll know your lines.

- Rest assured, I intend to pray over you and other friends who read this humble work. Together may we raise above the discord of suffering a glorious symphony of praise to our Savior.

Is the midnight closing round you?
Are the shadows dark and long?
Ask Him to come close beside you,
And He'll give you a new, sweet song.

He'll give it and sing it with you;
And when weakness lets it down,
He'll take up the broken cadence,
And blend it with His own.

And many a rapturous minstrel
Among those sons of light,
Will say of His sweetest music
"I learned it in the night."

And many a rolling anthem,
That fills the Father's home,
Sobbed out its first rehearsal,
*In the shade of a darkened room.**

*C. P., "Songs in the Night," in *The Shadow of the Rock and Other Poems*, ed. Edward Henry Bickersteth (London: Sampson Low, Marston, Low, & Searle, 1873), 173.

Acknowledgments

Thankful for These

I will certainly understand if you choose to skip these pages, but there are certain individuals I hope will linger here. And they know who they are. I want these dear friends to see how God used their prayers and efforts to help bring about this little volume. As a quadriplegic, I cannot raise my hands in applause, but if I could, I would stand and clap for the following.

Justin Taylor at Crossway tops the list. Actually, he shares that spot with Andrew Wolgemuth of Wolgemuth & Associates. Were it not for these two, you would be holding somebody else's book, and I'd be filing this stuff away in my journal. But Justin and Andrew saw something worthy in my idea to celebrate hymns of the faith through the painful seasons of life. I am grateful they thought it worth publishing.

I am thankful to John Nugent and the Executive Leadership Team at Joni and Friends for graciously excusing me from a zillion Zoom meetings so I might focus on writing. I'm especially grateful for their prayers. The leaders at Joni and Friends are aware that people with big limitations like mine need a lot of prayer.

My greatest help, however, came from the women who served as "my hands" in typing the manuscript—I talk, they type (especially when my voice dictating app freezes). Francie Lorey, Lisa Miehl, Kathren Martinez, Rainey Floreen, Christie Willis, and Catherine Cobb not only typed; they fed me lunch, emptied my leg bag, jumped on their laptops to do research, and cheered me on with their smiles and intercessions.

Extra thanks go to Catherine Cobb for shaping up this manuscript for delivery to Crossway (every author hopes a publisher will say, "Hey, these pages barely need tweaking!"). Catherine also served as a stellar research assistant. And thumbs-up goes to Joni and Friends' intern, Emily Mayfield, for helping with formatting and footnoting. She will go far when she embarks on her editing career.

My biggest cheerleader is always Ken Tada, my amazing husband. By the time you read this, we will have celebrated our fortieth wedding anniversary. Always my tireless advocate when I'm writing, I love the way he watches me from a distance, folds his arms, and gives that "I'm proud of you" look. What more could a wife ask?

Then there's my Pain Pals. This extraordinary group of men and women are my soulmates as they cleave to God and his word through intractable pain. We pals encourage one another by sharing faith-strengthening essays—works by G. D. Watson, Alexander Maclaren, Jon Bloom, John Piper, Thomas Brooks, John Bunyan, Samuel Rutherford, Charles Spurgeon, and I could go on. You have met a few pals on preceding pages, but I could fill bookshelves on how God has used their testimonies to freshen my heart when I'm low.

Finally, Pastor Bob Bjerkaas's sermons at our little PCA church are always brimming with true grit from God's word, and I can't tell you the times I wished I had hands to scribble his gems before his next point. Pastor Bob's sermons on the Psalms of Ascent, as well as his year-long series on the book of Job, reinforced the rebar in my faith, especially on Sundays when I sat "on top of pain" in church. I pray that one day he, too, may have the opportunity to deliver a manuscript to a publisher.

Oh, one more thing. I have heard people call me "the hymn lady," but I don't deserve that title. I give that honor to Bobbie Wolgemuth. We co-authored many books on hymns, and when we were together, never did we fail to harmonize on "O Worship the King." My last glimpse of Bobbie before she died of ovarian cancer was of her walking her neighborhood, wearing sneakers and a chemo cap, and singing "Trust and Obey." When you can do *that*, you earn the title "hymn lady."

Spirit of Jesus, thank you for blessing these precious ones. I reflect on their contributions and am reminded of 2 Corinthians 9:12: "For the ministry of this service is not only supplying the needs of the saints but is also overflowing in many thanksgivings to God." Yes, dear Lord, my heart is overflowing with gratitude for these friends. Surely you had them in mind when you inspired that verse.

Notes

1. James Nisbet, "Commentary on Daniel 6," Church Pulpit Commentary, StudyLight.org, accessed May 21, 2021, https://www.studylight.org/.
2. Malcolm Guite, "Beatus Vir: A Reflection on Psalm 1," in *David's Crown* (Atlanta: Canterbury Press, 2021). Used with permission.
3. Charles Spurgeon, "The Memorable Hymn, No. 2982," Spurgeon Gems, April 5, 1906, https://www.spurgeongems.org/.
4. Fanny Crosby, "All the Way My Savior Leads Me," 1875.
5. Oliver Sacks, *Musicophilia: Tales of Music and the Brain* (New York: Knopf, 2007), 158.
6. John Piper, "Singing, Suffering, and Scripture: How God Keeps Us through Song," message delivered at Sing! Global Conference, September 2, 2020, Nashville, TN; emphasis added.
7. Robert Frost, "Mending Wall," Poetry Foundation, accessed May 12, 2021, https://www.poetryfoundation.org/.
8. Ceri Jackson, "Aberfan: The Mistake That Cost a Village Its Children," BBC, October 21, 2016, https://www.bbc.co.uk/.
9. Jackson, "Aberfan."
10. Jackson, "Aberfan."
11. "Aberfan Disaster," Wikipedia, modified May 13, 2021, https://en.wikipedia.org/.
12. Flora Carr, "True Story behind *The Crown*'s Aberfan episode, as told by the survivors: 'I had nightmares for years,'" *Radio Times*, November 18, 2019, https://www.radiotimes.com/.

13. Geerhardus Vos, *Grace and Glory: Sermons Preached in the Chapel of Princeton Theological Seminary* (Grand Rapids, MI: Reformed Press, 1922), 95.

14. John Bunyan, *The Acceptable Sacrifice: The Excellency of a Broken Heart* (London: George Larkin, 1692).

15. Andrew Murray, source unknown.

16. Brad Stulberg, "How to Make Friends with Pain," *Outside* magazine, April 2, 2018, https://www.outsideonline.com/.

17. David Depp, "It Is Well with My Soul: Historical Origins of the Hymn and the Tune," October 27, 2015, YouTube, https://www.youtube.com/. See also "Horatio Gates Spafford: The Story behind the Hymn 'It Is Well with My Soul," Bethel Church Ripon, December 12, 2018, https://www.bethelripon.com/.

18. The concept in these last four sentences is not original to me. "To suffer well" is a phrase I've often heard John Piper use, and I extrapolated my reflections from his words.

19. Alexander Maclaren, "The Warrior Peace," Christian Classics Ethereal Library, accessed May 14, 2021, https://ccel.org/.

20. Chuck Bumgardner, "Samuel Rodigast: 'Whate'er My God Ordains Is Right,'" Religious Affections Ministries, modified February 21, 2011, https://religiousaffections.org/.

21. Bill Wymond, Derek Thomas, J. Ligon Duncan, "Whate're My God Ordains Is Right," *Hymns of the Faith*, podcast, January 6, 2008, https://www.fpcjackson.org/.

22. John Ruskin, "Streams in the Desert," Crosswalk.com, January 22, 2021, https://www.crosswalk.com/.

23. Rev. T. De Witt Talmage, "The Sword of Eleazar," in *Bright and Morning Star: Being a Sixth Series of Sermons* (London: William Nicholson & Sons, 1890), 99.

24. The idea of worshiping God as though facing a storm is not original to me. I regret I cannot recall the article or its author in order to give proper credit. But I thank him here.

25. Kevin Twit, "Anne Steele," Indelible Grace Hymn Book, accessed May 17, 2021, http://hymnbook.igracemusic.com/.

26. Anne Steele, "Thou Lovely Source of True Delight," HymnTime.com, modified April 15, 2021, http://www.hymntime.com/.

27. This description of God the Father was originally penned by Steve Estes. See *When God Weeps* (Grand Rapids, MI: Zondervan, 1997), n.p.

28. Ephesians 1:19–20.

29. St. Francis de Sales, "Francis de Sales," Daily Prayers, accessed June 2, 2021, https://www.daily-prayers.org/.

30. Charles Spurgeon, *Spurgeon's Sermons Volume 9: 1863*, Christian Classics Ethereal Library, accessed October 18, 2021, https://ccel.org/ccel/.

31. John Piper, *Don't Waste Your Life* (Wheaton, IL: Crossway, 2003).

32. See James 1:4.

33. Thomas Watson, "Thomas Watson's Choice Quotes on Prayer," Grace Gems, accessed July 16, 2021, https://www.gracegems.org/.

34. Charles Spurgeon, *According to Promise of Salvation, Life, and Eternity or, The Lord's Method of Dealing with His Chosen People* (Abbotsford, WI: Aneko Press, 2017), 71, 83–84, Kindle ed.

35. Bob Bjerkaas, "Psalms of Ascent," sermon delivered at Church in the Canyon, Calabasas, CA, 2021.

36. Percy Ainsworth, *The Pilgrim Church and Other Sermons* (London: Charles H. Kelly, 1909), 130–31.

37. Thomas Brooks, "Appendix to Memoir," *Works of Thomas Brooks*, vol. 1 (Carlisle, PA: Banner of Truth, 1980), lxiv.

38. Charles Spurgeon, "Leaning on Our Beloved," The Spurgeon Center, accessed October 19, 2021, https://www.spurgeon.org/.

39. Charles Spurgeon, *Beside Still Waters: Words of Comfort for the Soul*, ed. Roy H. Clarke (Nashville, TN: Thomas Nelson, 1999).

40. Sebastian Valfre, "St. Sebastian," The Martyrs' Sacrifice, accessed June 2, 2021, https://martyrsofthechurch.weebly.com/.

41. Augustine, "Top Quotes by Saint Augustine," Quote Master, accessed July 8, 2021, https://www.quotemaster.org/.

More for You

Books

Alcorn, Randy. *If God Is Good: Faith in the Midst of Suffering and Evil.* Colorado Springs, CO: Multnomah, 2009.

Bridges, Jerry. *Trusting God.* Colorado Spring, CO: NavPress, 2008.

Elliot, Elisabeth. *The Path of Loneliness: Finding Your Way through the Wilderness to God.* Repackaged edition. Grand Rapids, MI: Revell, 2007.

Guthrie, Nancy. *God Does His Best Work with Empty.* Carol Stream, IL: Tyndale Momentum, 2020.

Joni and Friends, *The Gospel in Hard Times: Study Guide with Leader's Notes.* Greensboro, NC: New Growth Press, 2019.

Lewis, C. S. *A Grief Observed.* London: Faber, 1961.

Piper, John. *Lessons from a Hospital Bed.* Wheaton, IL: Crossway, 2016.

Sittser, Gerald L. *A Grace Disguised: How the Soul Grows through Loss.* Grand Rapids, MI: Zondervan, 1995.

Somerville, Robert. *If I'm a Christian, Why Am I Depressed?* Maitland, FL: Xulon Press, 2014.

Tada, Joni Eareckson. *A Place of Healing: Wrestling with the Mysteries of Suffering, Pain, and God's Sovereignty.* Colorado Springs, CO: David C. Cook, 2010.

Tripp, Paul David. *Suffering: Gospel Hope When Life Doesn't Make Sense.* Wheaton, IL: Crossway, 2018.

Wolf, Jay, and Katherine Wolf. *Hope Heals: A True Story of Overwhelming Loss and an Overcoming Love.* Grand Rapids, MI: Zondervan, 2016.

Pamphlets Available at Joni and Friends

Gaining a Hopeful Spirit
God's Hand in Hardship
Making Sense of Suffering
Pain and Providence
A Thankful Heart

Music

Wolgemuth, Nancy DeMoss. *Psalms from the Heart: A Companion Resource for a 30-Day Walk with God in the Psalms.* Compact disc. Niles, MI: Revive Our Hearts, 2002.

———. *Be Still: Piano Meditations.* Compact disc. Niles, MI: Revive Our Hearts, 2013.

Scripture Index

About Joni and Friends

Joni and Friends is committed to bringing the gospel and practical resources to people living with disability around the globe. For over forty years, the ministry has been transforming people's understanding of disability in the community and in the church.

Joni and Friends offers church training, as well as Family Retreats, Marriage Getaways, Warrior Getaways, Wheels for the World, Respite@ Home, and Joni's House. Our Cause 4 Life internships provide a new generation of young people an opportunity to serve Jesus among families with special needs.

A disability can take many shapes and sizes. Whether grief, a deep sense of loss, pain, or an invisible chronic condition, Joni and Friends wants to share hope through your hardship. No matter what the limitation, if you have been touched by the insights in this book, or if you need help or prayer support, let us know how our teams may serve you.

Contact us at:

Joni and Friends
P.O. Box 3333
Agoura Hills, CA 91301

818-707-5664
joniandfriends.org
response@joniandfriends.org

About the Photography

The photography in this book was uniquely commissioned for this project. All of the photos were taken by Tim Kellner near Joni Eareckson Tada's home and at various locations along the West Coast, from Southern California to Seattle. Tim is a photographer and filmmaker based in New York. You can find more of his work on Instagram and YouTube.